Introduction

'Any spare change mate?' How often have you heard that? Many times I'm sure. It sometimes feels that you can't walk across any city centre, in any country, without being accosted by someone asking for money. Like you perhaps, I usually politely say no, fearing that my gift would be quickly spent on drugs or drink. But sometimes I relent and hand over some coins.

On one memorable evening in Blackpool I had quite a lengthy conversation with a homeless guy on the street. I'd flown up for a business meeting and was walking to my hotel after a pleasant meal, despite having eaten on my own. I guess I was missing home and happy to pause a while. Unlike so many, he wasn't begging, but offering something for sale. This is what caught my attention.

He had put together a collection of jokes, had them copied and stapled together by an accommodating local business and was offering them for sale for £2.50 each (the price of a copy of the *Big Issue*). I gave him £3.00 (he offered me change) and I congratulated him on his enterprise. He explained how he was angered by those who simply sat with their hand out.

Perhaps he'd failed to get a job selling the *Big Issue*, or perhaps he thought he would offer something different, that anyone might buy. What was clear though was that despite having fallen on hard times, he still had a degree of self-respect and felt that begging was beneath him. Of course he might have spent the money I gave him on drink or drugs, but I doubt it. We were fellow entrepreneurs, both working for ourselves, both trying to make our way in the world.

I kept his joke book for several years and often mentioned him when speaking at events. I wish I'd got his name, and learned more about his journey. I wonder if he will read this book and recognise himself.

This was not my first memorable experience of meeting someone who was homeless. Perhaps 30 years ago the company I co-owned produced a fundraising leaflet for Norwich charity St Martins. I had the idea of profiling some of the service users. I thought this would encourage people to give more generously.

I was introduced to someone living in a city centre hostel. He described how growing up in an abusive, dysfunctional family had led to him growing up with low self-esteem and recurring mental health problems. This he felt had contributed to the breakdown of his relationship with his partner, the loss of his job, home and just about everything else.

What he did not know, was that I too had grown up in a dysfunctional family. Yes, my father had been a respected figure in the market town where I grew up. But his struggle with his own demons had badly damaged his three children.

I grew up with no sense of self-worth and did badly at school. Only in later life, with lots of professional support and an incredibly tolerant and understanding wife, did I put

£1·25

ANY SPARE
CHANGE?

my past behind me and flourish in my career. Interviewing that resident of a St Martins hostel made me very aware that I could have so easily been overwhelmed by my past and found myself standing in his shoes.

Perhaps if more of us had the opportunity to have conversations like this, we would come to appreciate how lucky we are, and how close we all come at times to becoming homeless. It's said that most of us are just two pay packets away from the street. That's certainly true for those lacking family or friends able to afford to help them out. Society encourages us to live life to the limit, spending all that we earn. I think we need to be more honest with ourselves and not put ourselves at risk.

According the Office for National Statistics, over the last 20 years, house prices have risen by nearly 260%, while earnings rose by just 68% over the same period. Despite interest rates being low, that differential growth rate means many people cannot afford to buy a home. Rents are high too, particularly in London, where even a room in a shared flat can cost £700 a month. I paid £12,000 for my first house when I was 27 and now own a very nice home outright. Few in their twenties today have that opportunity.

Now let me tell you why I decided to write this book. Those two meetings with homeless people brought home to me, in a stark and vivid way, the simple fact that any of us could end up on the streets. I'm very aware that I, as I'm sure you, live my life in something of a bubble. I mix with people of similar age and background to myself. I worry about things that really don't matter, and my exposure to the gritty reality of homelessness is limited to being asked for money on the street.

In fact the link between rough sleeping and street begging is tenuous. Many rough sleepers are too proud or afraid to accost you in the street and ask for money. Others with a place to live choose street begging as a way to supplement their benefit payments. Yes, things are not always quite what they might seem.

Yet as a Quaker I have a strong desire to see a more equal world, where everyone has the same opportunity to realise their potential and live a safe, fulfilling life. Much of my career has been spent as a social entrepreneur. That's given me the opportunity to create ventures that support those excluded from opportunity. To me it's not enough to leave leading social change to others.

This book tells the story of a journey I made in the summer of 2019. I did not need to travel far, as everything I needed to see, and everyone I met along the way, was in Norwich. It could probably have been any city, because rough sleeping is seen as a problem in every large conurbation.

I set out to find out how and why people end up living on the streets. I wanted to discover what help was available to them and what you and I can do that is useful. It's natural to feel pity for the person sitting in a shop doorway who asks you for money. But is giving them some cash all you can do?

I was aware that you probably don't have the time to make this journey yourself, so I hope that sharing mine with you will help you better understand the complex issues surrounding rough sleeping in Norwich.

Inevitably there will be those among you who ask why this or that service provider was not included. Others will disagree with the route I took or feel that I showed bias in favour of St Martins. What I can say is that in researching this book, I've followed my instinct and, to my mind at least, followed a logical path.

Profits from your purchase of this book will go to St Martins, as they lead a consortium of organisations seeking to support people who find themselves on the street. But I've tried to be objective and present things as they appeared to me. I hope you find this story interesting, and when you have read it, feel you know just a little more about homelessness in Norwich.

Now let's start that journey.

1

Getting ready

'You're only as good as your last haircut.'
Fran Lebowitz

My journey really started sitting in my barber's chair on Upper King Street. The Attic Barbershop is on the second floor, above a café. The chair is by the window, so provides a view of the busy street outside. There's a bus stop opposite; I tend to make a mental note of the service number of each bus that stops there. This is one of my stranger traits.

That afternoon, rough sleeping and this book were on my mind. I knew that my barber Kyle had cut the hair of rough sleepers when he was learning his trade. It's apparently not uncommon for trainee barbers to use men on the street as guinea pigs. Hair grows just as quickly if you're sleeping in a shop doorway as it does if you live in a nice house. And if you live on the street, paying for a haircut is not going to be on your list of priorities.

I chose my moment well. Talking is easy while having your hair cut, but not advisable when your beard is being trimmed. So just as Kyle was about to move from my hair to my beard, I asked him to tell me what it was like cutting the hair of a rough sleeper. Men tend to talk about surprisingly personal things when in the barber's chair. It's why many barbers are trained in mental health first aid, so that they can respond helpfully to confessions of feeling depressed.

Kyle is a personable, cheerful young man. So I suspect he found it easier than many to approach someone in a shop doorway and offer to cut their hair. He'd then lead them back to the barbershop and start by washing their hair. The reasons for this are pretty obvious, but it's a particularly intimate activity. The last person to wash my hair was my late mother more than 50 years ago. It might well be the same for these guys.

Then they were always asked how they'd like their hair cut. You and I will be accustomed to being asked to make simple choices. But if you live on the street, you're more likely to be kicked than offered the opportunity to make a decision. So it's perhaps no surprise that as Kyle cut their hair, they tended to open up and talk about their lives.

Some talked about the circumstances that had led to them living rough. Relationship breakdown was a common feature. This can not only lead to eviction from the family home, but estrangement from often quite young children. To lose your home is one thing, but to lose contact with your family is something quite different. It's no surprise that poor mental health often accompanies rough sleeping.

One person stood out from the rest in Kyle's mind. A man of about 50, he was well spoken and polite. He talked about the business he'd started and run for a number of years. Like so many entrepreneurs, he'd secured his business borrowing against his house. It's often the only way a bank will lend to a growing company.

Things went well for a few years, and then things changed for the worse. Through no fault of his own, a few bad debts, a fall in sales and perhaps delaying cutting back on costs led to the bank calling in the loan. He lost his house, his wife left him as well and after outstaying the welcome of a friend who let him sleep on their sofa, he found himself on the streets.

His story illustrated well the sad fact that homelessness can happen to anyone. Yes, drug and alcohol addiction and poor mental health are often the consequence of homelessness, but not necessarily the cause.

Kyle and I talked more about this book. How am I going to make this a meaningful exploration of a highly emotive subject? Only by truly understanding the problem can any of us hope to influence it. We're confronted daily by street beggars, yet these may not be quite as deserving as they first appear. (You can earn a good tax free living begging in a city centre.)

Another person I told about my plan, Chris, suggested I take part in one of the organised charity sleep-outs organised by Norwich charity The Benjamin Foundation. This, he explained, would give me the chance to experience what rough sleeping was really like. But would it? Real rough sleeping is not organised, safe or with the convenience of a nearby toilet (something rather important when you are in your sixties).

Raising money by being sponsored to take part in an organised sleep-out is to be encouraged. But I think I'd be doing a disservice to those this book aims to help to assume that the real thing is anything like as comfortable as an organised event. I decided that I would speak to as many people as I could, but that I'd not try in any way to simulate the rough sleeping experience. I have a nice home, a loving wife and, whenever I need to sleep, a warm comfortable bed.

As you would expect, I also spent time talking with Jan Sheldon, CEO of St Martins. After all, as her organisation's website says, they are 'helping the homeless build a better life in Norwich and Norfolk'. I'd got to know Jan over the past year, having been introduced to her at an event. Having shown interest, I was invited to join an Advisory Group, which meets a couple of times a year to, well, advise. It's a useful sounding board, off which to bounce strategic ideas.

Quite early on, Jan picked me up on my use of language. Rough sleeping and homelessness are quite different and while all rough sleepers are homeless, not all homeless people have to resort to sleeping rough. She went on to explain how many people rely on friends and relatives to put them up when they lose their home. This is usually a temporary arrangement, but the pressure of having someone sleeping on your sofa can put real strain on even a close friendship. Many also find themselves sleeping in their car, at least if they have a car that is!

Jan offered to take me on a tour of the St Martins services in Norwich. This I thought would be a welcome introduction to the world I was planning to explore. She is good company and after all, St Martins will benefit from the income this book generates. A date was arranged and late one morning, I found my way to Webster Court, a residential care home for those aged over 50.

We then drove to Bishopbridge House, a 30-bed hostel which is often the first port of call for someone seeking respite from life on the streets. The rooms are all en suite and look surprisingly comfortable. There's one room with four camp beds. This is where you sleep if no room is available and you literally have nowhere else to go.

Highwater House followed. This is a 22-bed unit that will take you if you drink, do drugs or have a mental health problem. You can drink on site, although obviously you can't take drugs. Next door is the 'Under One Roof' service, where people can learn new skills. The words written on the whiteboard in one of the training rooms during a session about wellbeing and self-esteem impressed me.

Finally we crossed the city again to visit the Dibden Road Hostel. Again, I had a quick tour of the building, this time interrupted by one resident who wanted to show Helen, my guide, his badly swollen foot. Their conversation reminded me that whatever your view on homelessness, there is a frailty and vulnerability to the men who live here.

Over the next few days I arranged to return to each location to meet the manager and interview some of the residents. This was going to shape my journey through the world of homelessness in Norwich. But first, I needed to develop an understanding of the big picture.

2

The big picture

'You cannot feed the hungry on statistics.'
David Lloyd George

Rough sleeping is not a new problem. In the years that followed the Napoleonic War, which ended in 1815, many men were discharged from the Army and unable to find work or accommodation. They slept rough, often forming camps with others, finding food and casual work where and when they could.

Poverty and famine in Ireland in the 19th century also led to many coming across to England in search of work. Many of these men too ended up living on the streets. The Vagrancy Act (1824) was introduced in response to this dramatic increase in rough sleeping, forcing those with no home to keep moving. To spend more than one night in any one place was a criminal act. One month's hard labour was the penalty for those found guilty of vagrancy.

Those living in this way became known as tramps, because they were always walking from one place to the next, or tramping. Even 50 years ago, when I was a teenager in rural East Suffolk, it was not unusual to see what we used to call 'gentleman of the road'. They would often find casual work and shelter on farms, and be given cast off clothing to replace the rags they arrived in.

One man I remember lived in the woods and spent his days sitting on the grass verge at a road junction near Friston. We all knew him and he would wave back as we passed. Rumour had it that years ago he had killed his girlfriend and been to prison. He chose to live that way and a number of nearby residents would give him food and keep an eye on him.

But today most who find themselves homeless gravitate to the cities and larger towns. While the Vagrancy Law remains in force, people are no longer punished for sleeping rough. After all, life on the streets is tough enough in itself; a police or prison cell is comfortable by comparison. Most that become homeless quickly discover that in a city you can easily find food, and places where you can have a shower and wash your clothes.

Begging is of course also an option, but not one likely to make you popular with others on the street. One former rough sleeper told me, with some anger in his voice, how professional beggars made life difficult for those who really did not have anywhere to sleep at night. Too many of us take the outstretched hand at face value. Giving to beggars can salve our conscience.

For those with an addiction to feed, urban areas offer greater opportunity for shoplifting and other petty crime. Surprisingly, it is their fellow rough sleepers who most often get mugged on the street. One man told me that he always lied when asked how much money he'd made begging that day. Banknotes were always tucked in his sock, where they were hard for a thief to find, even when he was asleep in a doorway.

Most evenings, on Haymarket in the very centre of Norwich, volunteers provide free food and drink to those that queue here for a free meal. There can be 80 or 90 people here some nights, and as some who've eaten here tell me, it's not very safe. One man I met, whose story is in Chapter Four, was stabbed by someone else in the queue.

I was keen to understand the issues and challenges surrounding rough sleeping. It remains as much a concern today as perhaps it was 200 years ago. Successive Governments have introduced legislation, most recently the Homelessness Reduction Act 2017, but people are still sleeping rough.

To find out more, I visited both City Hall and the local Job Centre, which is operated by the Department for Work and Pensions, which of course handles claims for benefits. At both I was welcomed and had interesting conversations. Officers at both said that they would prefer not to be quoted directly in the book.

Most organisations in the public sector have specialist teams to manage their external communication. I chose not to ask for an official comment; instead I attended a meeting of the Greater Norwich Homelessness Forum, where I had the chance to hear the topic being debated by a wide range of local stakeholders.

Now over the last 30 or more years I've had countless dealings with people in the public sector. Elected members can in my experience be both ardent supporters, or simply not understand the opportunity. Officers on the other hand can be more focused on their pension than your project, resisting change and thwarting innovation.

This is changing though. There are a growing number of public sector mutuals; effectively cooperatives that have spun out of local government and the NHS. Financially accountable and often very innovative, they often cut across traditional discipline boundaries to deliver services that put the user first, rather than the funder.

None I met in Norwich was working for organisations that have left the relative safety of the public sector. But this change in approach by many across the UK has had a ripple effect everywhere. In an environment where Government policy shapes funding, it can be so easy to go with the flow, make sure the right boxes are ticked, and steer well clear of any risk. But none I'd met could be accused of that.

The housing officers I met at City Hall took their jobs seriously and were both well informed and focused on making a difference. One talked about rough sleepers with whom he'd pause for a chat on his way to work. He listened to what they said and the things he heard I think influenced his decision-making. I saw compassion rather than sympathy, and a can-do attitude rather than the more traditional jobsworth stalling.

It was fascinating to learn that a member of the local DWP team often goes out at six in the morning, with the Pathways outreach team, to talk to rough sleepers. He makes sure they are claiming the benefits they're entitled to and takes a very practical approach to helping them with the necessary paperwork.

If you haven't got a bank account, and many on the street don't, he helps them open an account with the local credit union. The Job Centre can be used as an address if you need one, and because Universal Credit is paid in arrears, you can get an advance straight away.

It was a revelation to learn that you might be sleeping in a quiet piece of city woodland and wake at dawn to find a man from the Job Centre crouched beside you offering to help you claim your benefits. Some, perhaps those who still see rough sleeping as the consequence of foolishness, find this approach overly generous. But the fact is that nobody sets out to become homeless and sleep rough. It can take little to tip many of us on to a helter-skelter of bad luck that can lead to life on the street. Remember that for every person rough sleeping, there are perhaps 40 or 50 living in temporary accommodation, with the very real risk that tomorrow, they will have nowhere to sleep.

It would be fair to say that my research for this book delivered a good number of wow moments, as I discovered just how far people from all walks of life, including the public sector, will go to help someone who, quite literally, is on their uppers.

But let's not paint too rosy a picture. I mentioned earlier that I attended a meeting of the Greater Norwich Homelessness Forum. This brings together the city council, and the two district councils that adjoin it. Add to them local charities, such as St Martins and the YMCA, probation and on this occasion a fascinating guy from a faith-led organisation that provides accommodation in partnership with local churches.

We met in Broadland Council's Chamber, where members do politics and the public often come along to listen, lobby and at times, protest. Once we were all seated and the presentations started, I quickly discovered that acronyms abound in the homelessness world as they do across the entire public sector.

For example I worked out that TA means temporary accommodation and CBL means choice-based lettings. In other words, the online bidding system that lets those on the council's housing list pitch for the properties they'd like to live in.

There were others too, but clearly all those present part from me were familiar with these acronyms, while I had to work them out. I wondered how often someone from outside the world of homelessness attended these meetings.

I won't bore you with what was discussed, other than to say that what was being shared was far more interesting than the style with which it was presented. I guess I've spoken at too many events to not notice when others fail to fully engage with their audience. I had five minutes at the end, to speak about this book. I needed reassurance that I was not wasting my time. I leave you to decide that!

Some of the statistics shared were particularly interesting. The single biggest cause of homelessness was the termination of a private sector tenancy. This could be for a wide range of reasons, but it suggested that private sector landlords are far less tolerant than councils or housing associations.

The second biggest cause of homelessness was when friends and family could no longer tolerate you sleeping on the sofa, floor or if you're lucky, in their spare room. Just as things can get tense when adult children remain living in the family home, they get tense even faster if the lodger is your drinking buddy or just a friend you've taken pity on.

Next was domestic abuse, perhaps the biggest cause of women becoming homeless and normally, when a relationship fails, it is the man who leaves while the woman and any children remain; at least, providing they can still pay the rent.

It came as no surprise that most who become homeless are aged 18 to 45 years old. It's the period in your life when you're building your future, and your rent or mortgage payments represent a significant proportion of your income. It's also a time when you have little by way of savings to fall back on. By comparison in your 50s and older, income is often higher and as children leave home, costs tend to be lower.

The Homelessness Reduction Act was big on the agenda. Nationally £32m had been allocated by Government to a new rough sleeping initiative to provide 1,750 new beds. Of this, £400,000 has been secured by Norwich City Council. A city centre building will be converted to provide a new hostel, where you can stay for three days. This will give the local Pathways team time to work with people to find either a longer term hostel place, or even a council flat.

That is if planning consent for change of use is granted. As I was writing this book there was a flurry of local opposition to the application. One objector stated: 'this proposal would result in an increase in crime and disorder in the local area,' while another said it might attract drug dealers to the area. Both are typical fears expressed by those concerned about finding themselves living close to homeless people. Yet of course many do so already and don't realise as many popular rough sleeping spots are in residential areas.

Because the Government funding for this also covers the first year's revenue cost, it will be possible to accommodate those with no recourse to public funds. Because most hostel places are funded by housing benefits, those not entitled to benefits cannot be accommodated.

This new homelessness legislation is quite interesting. It came into law in April 2018 and places greater responsibility of local authorities to support those at risk of, or who have become homeless. The focus on preventing homelessness occurring is new. I wonder how many people at risk of losing their home think to contact their local council?

Reading Shelter's guidance on the Act, it is reassuringly pragmatic for what could so easily have been demanding legislation. The onus is on helping those at risk of losing their homes, not preventing that loss. A Council clearly cannot intervene if a private landlord is threatening eviction for good reason. Success is defined as helping the person find new accommodation with at least six months security of tenure.

Those being made unintentionally homeless, i.e. through no fault of their own, are supported as a priority, over those who have contributed to their eviction, perhaps by running up rent arrears. This is logical, but does not allow for the fact that some struggle to maintain their tenancy because of poor mental health. I guess in these cases, people are referred to those in the health and charity sector able to help them. I noted that the local NHS Clinical Commissioning Group, the organisation that funds health, is a member of the forum.

As you would expect, this new Act also sets performance targets. What became clear when I attended the

Homelessness Reduction Forum was that this new Act has prompted councils to take a more proactive approach to homelessness. No longer should people wait until they are in crisis before they talk to their council. One officer talked about making home visits to those at risk. This has to be a good move.

Norfolk is one of the places where attempts to create a unitary authority have failed. We still have Norfolk County Council and seven district, borough and city councils. Those that surround Norwich, South Norfolk and Broadland are merging their teams, although politically they remain different authorities. It makes total sense for them to partner with the city council, as most who end up rough sleeping in the wider area find their way to Norwich, where most of the services are located.

A few days after the meeting, I had a coffee with Maria, the Homelessness Services Manager for St Martins. We talked about the changing legislation and how the Pathways service she helped develop came about.

Maria

First joining the team as a volunteer, Maria quickly decided that this was a place she wanted to work. She's now been with St Martins 18 years and clearly loves her work. When St Martins were invited to tender for a council contract to support those sleeping rough, she had the courage to challenge the brief.

This led to an invitation to co-design a new service and Pathways Norwich was the result. Usefully, Pathways is a true partnership between a number of agencies and charities. This takes away the need to compete for funding and encourages collaboration. It also refreshingly means that the vulnerable person, experiencing life on the streets gets seamless support, rather than being passed from one provider to another as used to happen in the past.

Pathways has a city centre office and sends out an outreach team early each morning to all the places where rough sleepers tend to spend the night. I mentioned earlier how one of the DWP team goes out periodically to offer help claiming benefits. Mental health specialists and prescribing nurses also go out, taking healthcare to those who find going to a surgery an ordeal.

We talked too about the nightly soup run that can see 80 people queuing up in the city centre for free food. Maria made the point that there are plenty of places you can get fed in the city centre. She said that feeding people in the street does little for their dignity or sense of self-respect. As I'd already learned, it's not the safest place to go if you're in need of food.

The appropriately named Pathways Service delivers just that: a pathway you can follow when you want to stop sleeping on the street. I'm sure most cities have something similar, but I'm rather impressed by what I've seen in Norwich. People enter the pathway when they either visit the Pathways office, or are met on the street by one of the outreach team. A hostel bed is usually available and once settled there, you're helped to make plans for the future.

One thing I found interviewing people on the pathway is that the planning for the future actually means next week, or maybe the week after. When leaving rough sleeping, you are focused on survival and unlikely to be thinking about long term plans. You simply want to escape from the horror of your current situation.

Support is there to deal with money, addictions, mental or other health problems. As you begin to recover, you are invited to move to a more permanent hostel place, and from here, perhaps a year or more later, you can secure a council flat. Some have rent arrears to deal with, but that rarely stops you getting housed. After all, your rent is paid by DWP if you are not yet working.

Many at this point start selling the *Big Issue*, about which I will write later, and many in time get a job. St Martins and others offer a range of courses and help for those seeking employment. Most of the front line workers I met have examples of people who may have suffered a spectacular fall from a professional role, then bounced back a year or so later to a similar job. While poverty is at the heart of homelessness, it would be wrong to assume that only the poor can find themselves sleeping on the streets.

Maria told me about an initiative being piloted in Norwich. Housing First is where you put someone straight into a council flat and provide pretty intensive support (typically one support worker to seven tenants) to help them deal with any issues while settling down in what will become their long-term home. We all know how much better we feel when at home, so getting someone off the streets and quickly into a flat makes sense.

From the council's perspective, they know that the new tenant has lots of support and so is very likely to become a good tenant. It also takes pressure off hostel accommodation, which is costly to run and may be in short supply in some places.

I was reminded of an earlier conversation, when I learned that some people may not have the skills or experience to manage a tenancy. If you're raised in care, have spent time in the armed forces or prison, you may be quite institutionalised and simply not know how to cope living on your own.

As I was writing this chapter, someone I know commented that the Government had promised to solve the problem of homelessness. They suggested that because it still exists, the Government had failed. That I think is an unfair expectation. There has always been homelessness and people have always found themselves sleeping rough.

This is not going to ever stop happening. The problems that cause homelessness will always exist. All we can hope to do is to become competent and compassionate in how society deals with those who have tumbled out of job, home and relationships to suffer the indignity and dangers of life on the streets.

3

A strange coincidence

'*We are continually shaped by the forces of coincidence.*'
Paul Auster

Fresh from my research, I ventured out to meet one of the Trustees of St Martins. I thought this would be a good starting point. I also knew I would have to speak with people from other organisations. I wanted to understand.

I'd been surprised that so much had been written about homelessness. Clearly the Homelessness Reduction Act, which came into law in 2018, made it the responsibility of councils to 'prevent and relieve homelessness'. But making something a legal obligation does not mean the problem goes away. In the past, I've seen how passing a law or writing a strategy simply shifts responsibility from one place to another, but does nothing to actually address the problem.

If you have become homeless and moved into the city, then you are supposed to be helped by the council for where you came from. But if you're even 20 miles away, living rough, how can they possibly know? And perhaps more importantly, where can they place you when there is a national housing shortage? I read in my local paper that in Norfolk there are more than 200 children placed with their parent(s) in bed and breakfast or hostel accommodation.

And then of course there is the simple fact that many become homeless because they ran up rent arrears, or behaved antisocially and were evicted. You can't just put someone with a history of antisocial behaviour in a flat and expect them to live differently this time. You need to work with them to understand, and help them overcome the problems that made them homeless in the first place.

Janka, a Trustee

So it was with these thoughts on my mind that I met Janka for a coffee. Young, bright, highly qualified and keen to make a difference, Janka was certainly not a typical charity trustee. According to the National Council for Voluntary Organisations (NCVO), the average trustee is white, male and aged over 60. Janka certainly did not fit that profile!

Many charity trustees are in my experience even older and so almost inevitably find leading change difficult. Yet change is increasingly what the charity sector is facing, as statutory funding continues to be reduced and the need for services continues to grow. We need more young trustees.

When we met, Janka was coming to the end of her first three-year term on the Board. Her job was different now, having moved from Norfolk Community Advice Network to become Head of Operations at Norwich-based Mancroft Advice Project (MAP). She wondered if she could still be as useful now her job had changed.

Her previous role was working with organisations providing free debt and benefits advice, and mediating in cases where a tenancy is at risk because of rent arrears. This is really important, as despite councils having a statutory obligation to house those who find themselves on the street, they can still evict you. If they consider that you have made yourself intentionally homeless or if you have 'no recourse to public funds' those obligations don't apply.

The majority of rented accommodation is provided by private landlords. So if you are a 'difficult' tenant in their eyes – perhaps you haven't paid your rent, perhaps you argued with your neighbours, all of which may be because of poor mental health or antisocial behaviour – you can find yourself out on the street. This may seem fair to you, but often those evicted are vulnerable, struggling to cope and grew up without anyone showing them how to budget, or deal with bureaucracy. This may be especially true of people who grew up in care, without a parent to learn from.

In her current job, Janka manages the delivery of support services to young people aged between 11 and 25. Her organisation's vision is that 'all young people will know what it is to be valued, and that they will have the support and information they need to make a successful transition to adulthood'.

While few youngsters find themselves on the streets, many, in particular care leavers, struggle to find a place to live. We all know that in fact, it's difficult for any young person leaving home to find affordable accommodation of their own. It's why so many remain living reluctantly with their parents until they have saved enough to move out.

Navigating the benefits minefield is difficult for most

people. For those experiencing homelessness, it can be even more challenging. St Martins offers benefits advice to those using its services. I suspect that Janka's involvement means that the advice offered is particularly well informed. Her day job may have changed, but I suspect that her network remains invaluable.

Of course St Martins is not the only show in town, but it is certainly the largest provider, with more than 100 beds. There are other organisations I need to meet and speak with. And of course homelessness is a national problem, not just something that happens on my doorstep in Norwich. Where do I draw the line, I asked myself? How far afield should this journey take me?

With this on my mind, I said goodbye to Janka and walked across the city centre to a networking event I'd booked to attend. I was not really in the mood to speak with strangers, but decided my mood would not be improved by ducking out, so I went. The rain didn't help, and on arrival I had to clean the raindrops from my glasses so that I could at least see who I was talking too.

Benjamin

I was the first to arrive, and so had a few moments to reflect before others started to enter the room. One young man was busy on his phone, avoiding eye contact and conversation. I chose him to speak with, but got it badly wrong. He said he was Aspergic and that this was a genetic thing, not as I had politely suggested, anything to do with high IQ.

This was not a good start, but I was saved by the start of the formal part of the evening: three short presentations. A late arrival, a man with smiling eyes, stood beside me and listened to the speakers. When they finished, conversation with him was inevitable. After the usual exchange of views about what we had just heard, we asked what each other did and found we were both writers.

It was at this point that things became really interesting. He asked what I was working on at the moment and I replied, a book about homelessness. 'What, really?' he said. 'I slept rough for a time in Brixton.' I stepped back and looked at him again. From an Asian family, he was perhaps in his late 30s and did not look like someone who'd slept rough. I was suddenly glad I'd decided to go along that evening. His name was Benjamin.

We talked some more and he told me his story. I wondered as he talked how many others could tell the same story. He had been thrown out of the family home by his father, with no money and nowhere to go. His mother and siblings had chosen not to get involved and so he had no recourse but to sleep out in the streets.

Even in that situation Benjamin remained a young man with principles. He promised himself three things: he would never beg, never steal and never do drugs. He'd seen others go down that path and did not want to go there himself.

He had a little money and there was a soup kitchen in Brixton where he could get a free meal. Despite sleeping rough he looked after himself, kept himself looking clean and tidy, and one day bumped into a cousin who invited him round. The cousin knew he'd left the family home, but did not know Benjamin was sleeping rough, or so he thought.

The invitation was for pizza and beer, and Benjamin

contributed a five pound note he'd been holding on to for months as he wanted to pay his way. It proved to be a good investment. At the end of the evening the cousin went upstairs and returned with bedding. He'd clearly realised Benjamin's plight and, without asking, offered a place to stay.

This marked a turning point in Benjamin's life. Soon after he found a job, then a flat of his own, and finally a partner, with whom he'd recently moved to Norfolk where he'd written a book. You know it can sometimes only take one act of kindness to turn a life round.

Meeting Benjamin really brought home to me the fact that any one of us can become homeless. Like Benjamin, I had an unhappy upbringing. I too had a less than ideal relationship with my father. Looking back I remembered one incident in my own teenage years that could so easily have resulted in me becoming homeless like Benjamin.

My father told me one day, as I was going out, that I had better get my hair cut before I returned that evening or I'd not be staying. Of course I didn't as in my view, my hair was far from long and anyway, it was my hair, on my head and my decision how often to get it cut. I guess I was about 16 at the time.

When I got home my father had already started drinking. This was not unusual, but it meant that his rage that my hair remained uncut was greater than it might have otherwise been. I was told to 'get out until you've had a haircut', so I obliged and walked out of the back door. I had some change in my pocket, but not enough for a haircut, and anyway it was evening, and the barbers shop in town was closed until the morning.

I sat in the far corner in the garden wondering what to do. Upset at what she had just witnessed, my mother had spoken to my father and struck a deal. I could return to the family home that night if I allowed her to cut my hair. She didn't take much off my hair that evening; just enough to give my father the victory he wanted. I did get it cut properly the next day and so reluctantly gave in to his wishes.

Had either my father or I been angrier that evening, I could have walked further than a corner of the garden. My mother would then have not found me so easily and I would probably have stayed out all night. I doubt then that I would have returned in the morning. I probably would not have wanted to go to college unwashed and dishevelled from a night in a shop doorway. Yes, it really is that easy to become homeless.

In some ways I envied Benjamin because I had lacked the courage to keep walking when I was thrown out that evening. Of course it is quite likely that he could not have appeased his father with something as simple as a haircut.

Now you might be thinking that to become homeless because of an argument over a haircut is trivial and stupid. But the fact is, that it can be the smallest thing that can tip an already unhappy relationship into the catastrophe that is rough sleeping. Like me, Benjamin did not get along with his father. He didn't tell me what had caused his father to throw him out. It didn't matter. But unlike me, Benjamin had not given in and, as a result, became homeless.

That common experience, though, created an instant bond between us. We'll meet again I'm sure and perhaps get to know each other better. It is that same bond that later

I learn can create a sense of camaraderie between fellow rough sleepers. I was struck by the strange coincidence that he should have experienced homelessness, just as I was writing about it. Perhaps we were meant to meet.

That sense of connection I felt with Benjamin is something many with a common experience share. It's why we live among people like ourselves, and why we join clubs, associations or go to church. In a world of more than seven billion people, we need to feel we belong to a far smaller unit. So without thinking we organise ourselves into tribal communities.

The anthropologist Robin Dunbar suggested that we are happiest when within a community of fewer than 150 people. I suspect most of us have a social circle, excluding perhaps Facebook 'friends', of fewer than 150. Malcolm Gladwell, in his book *The Tipping Point*, suggested that when an organisation goes beyond 150 employees, it becomes harder to manage and social problems can arise.

It's certainly why those who find themselves homeless often buddy up with others in the same boat. Later I met someone who had been part of a community of twelve people sleeping rough in the same car park each night. They shared money and food and kept an eye on each other's meagre possessions. Even when stripped of home, income and family, we form close bonds with others with whom we have much in common.

Nick

The next day, I'd arranged to meet Nick, another Trustee of St Martins. We met in the same café where the day before

I'd spoken with Janka. At first appearance, Nick fitted the profile of a typical charity trustee. He's white, male and over 60. But unlike so many, Nick is progressive, connected and forward looking. He also bought me a coffee, which was nice.

Talking with Nick was fascinating. He'd been a city councillor for many years, and had been nominated by the council to join the St Martins Board some 29 years ago. It was, he told me, the practice in the early 1990s for the council to place a representative onto the Board of charities it regularly funded.

This made sense, as it meant that they were well placed to be aware of and influence the strategy of those they were part-funding. I like to think that this also meant more informed decision making in the Council Chamber. Nick is also a Trustee of the Norwich Historic Churches Trust, another charity with close links with the city council.

Nick could have stepped down from the Board when he stood down as a councillor. But he chose to remain because he said, 'the work they do is so important and I felt I could continue to contribute, even when no longer on the council'.

Nick is something of a historian, so we talked about the early days of the charity. 'St Martin,' he told me, 'is the patron saint of beggars, which is why the charity was so named.' The first night shelter was a redundant city centre church. It only accepted single homeless men who were accommodated in the nave of the former church, with little privacy.

Washing facilities were, he said, rudimentary, with nowhere to prepare hot food either. The shelter later moved to another former church in Oak Street which had 24 beds, which were often not enough, so some slept in chairs, on benches or the floor. He lent me an appeal leaflet, produced around the turn of the century, when funding was being sought to open a new direct access hostel, Bishopbridge House. The leaflet listed a pretty impressive group of supporters, including the bishop, local judges, chief constable, four local MPs and Stephen Fry.

Nick gave me some press cuttings from this time. One profiled people who were using the night shelter back in 2000. One pictured a 36 year old man with an unusual name. This enabled me to search for him on line. I soon found him, as he'd recently been up before the courts for shoplifting in Portsmouth. The report said he was of no fixed abode. Not every life is turned round by St Martins.

There was understandable concern from those living around the proposed site of Bishopbridge House. A number of public meetings were held in the neighbourhood, to allow residents to better understand what was planned. As Nick said at the time, 'our experience with our existing hostels is that they do not cause neighbourhood problems'. Bishopbridge House opened in 2002 and remains what St Martins call a 'direct access' hostel. That means it's where you go when found to be rough sleeping. St Martins staff tour the city centre early each morning speaking with those they discover sleeping rough. Some refer themselves and that's fine, I'm told. What's most important is to get someone off the street and somewhere safe.

I asked Nick how else things had changed over the years he's been involved. 'We're seeing younger people these day,' he explained, 'and men who have served in the armed forces and ex-prisoners.' Of course homelessness can strike at any age, becoming a way of life for some, and an unhappy episode in an otherwise happy life for others.

Not surprisingly, addiction has always been a problem, with more drug users today than 20 years ago, when alcohol was the main problem. It's hard to know which comes first, the addiction or homelessness. Mental health problems are also on the increase, with many support services seeing an increase in demand, and a decrease in statutory funding.

Talking with Nick I was reminded of Norfolk author George Borrow's book *The Romany Rye*. Written in 1857, it describes how he took to the road, travelling as a vagrant and sleeping under hedges. As I've already mentioned, when I was young, you would occasionally see what we then called 'gentlemen of the road.' Today, most who find themselves rough sleeping gravitate to the cities, where there is a better chance of finding food, clothing and people willing to give you a few coins.

But perhaps more than anything else, I was struck by how close I'd been to becoming a rough sleeper. Thanks to Benjamin I was reminded of that almost forgotten episode in my youth.

As our conversation helped me realise, I'd been close to becoming homeless myself. Perhaps you too have had similar experiences. I think it's one of the reasons why homelessness is such an emotive subject.

4

Read all about it

'I wanted to be an editor or a journalist, I wasn't really interested in being an entrepreneur, but I soon found I had to become an entrepreneur in order to keep my magazine going.'
Richard Branson

No book about rough sleeping would be complete without saying something about the *Big Issue*. Founded in 1991 by John Bird and Gordon Roddick, it was a response to the growing problem of homelessness in London. Now with a seat in the House of Lords, John Bird grew up in poverty and had first-hand experience of being homeless. But he'd also attended art school, and it was his creativity that led to the unlikely partnership with Gordon Roddick and the launch of the *Big Issue*.

Today you can buy your weekly copy of the *Big Issue* in every large town and city. The magazine has done more than any other to raise awareness of homelessness in Great Britain. Vendors are given a badge, five free copies of the magazine and a pitch from which to sell them. The income from these first few copies allows them to buy more copies, for which they pay 50% of the cover price. These they then have to sell to recoup their investment and make a profit.

The *Big Issue*'s mantra is 'a hand up, not a hand out'. Vendors bear the financial risk of not selling all the copies they buy. I'd met John Bird a few times, and been impressed by the way the magazine helped people earn their way out of poverty. As importantly, the magazine also prompts positive exchanges between vendors and passers-by. By now I was learning that something as simple as a casual conversation could make all the difference to someone isolated by poverty from mainstream society.

So intent on buying a copy and speaking with a vendor, I walked across the city centre. I did not have to go far to find someone wearing the familiar badge, and carrying an armful of copies. I made my purchase and offered to buy him a coffee if he had time to talk to me. 'I'm busy right now,' he told me, 'because Monday is my best day and I have these copies still to sell.' He showed me his stock of copies in his bag.

That in itself told me a lot about the work ethic of those selling the *Big Issue*. Here was a man who saw it as a real job, which of course it is. We agreed to meet later in the week and over a coffee, Mark told me his story. It was fascinating, at times a little shocking, but above all, encouraging. He would make a great poster boy for the magazine, as he really had used it to gain a hand up from poverty.

Mark

When we spoke, Mark had that week applied for a full-time job driving a forklift truck. He finally felt his life had reached a point where he could hold down a full-time job again. That was something he'd not done for a few years. As we drank our coffees, he told me why.

Mark was born on the coast and had worked as a car valeter for a seaside taxi company. 'The work was good,' he told me, 'and it's surprising what you find people leave behind in a cab.' He talked of returning the jewellery and mobile phones he found under car seats. Sometimes he got a cash reward, and at other times just the satisfaction of having helped reunite someone with an item of sentimental value.

A passion for cars and some less than ideal company had led to him stealing cars, removing valuable parts which his friends then bought from him, before dumping the car on the edge of town. He'd not set out to steal cars, but had found it a lot easier to remove a catalytic converter when confident the car's owner was not going to turn up and find him underneath their car.

This gave him more money in his pocket that his job at the taxi company and for a time, life was good. But inevitably he was picked up by the police, and found himself serving a prison sentence. This he said was horrible, and when he was released in 2004 his partner, home and young son had gone, leaving him on his own with no job, no money and little hope. I was pleased to learn that his now grown up son and he were back in touch and often met up. That is not always the case as I discovered later on.

Mark's brother lives in Norwich and had recently had a heart attack. Mark came to the city to stay with him for a bit, and help him look after his two sons. He still had no job and his benefits would be affected if he lived with his brother all the time, so he spent three nights a week there, and the rest of the week sleeping nearby in a tent. It was early summer, and he found that sleeping out was not too bad.

He knew about the *Big Issue* and needing to make some money, went along to their city base and signed up. He told me that there are more than 50 vendors in Norwich, with each allocated a pitch from which to sell. Joining the vendor team is surprisingly simple. You register, get an official vendor badge, a pitch and five copies to sell.

Mark sold them and invested the proceeds in buying more. Selling the *Big Issue* gave him something to do and some much needed income. But it also gave him back his sense of self-respect and a return to the daily routine of going to work.

There is universality to selling the *Big Issue*. You don't need specialist training, just a smile and willingness to engage passers-by in conversation. If you can do it, you soon sell your copies and get some more. If you can't, well you have to try something else.

The job can be surprisingly lucrative. Mark told me that in a good week, with a decent pitch and nice weather, he could sell up to 250 copies of the magazine. Even on a bad week, he will sell 50 copies, and like any self-employed person, the more hours he can put in, the greater the potential income.

But as Mark told me, not everyone who starts with the

Big Issue continues. There is a crack cocaine problem in Norwich and for some, the temptation to spend money on their next fix proves impossible to resist. I guess some take their free copies, make £12.50 then spend it on drugs. I'm told £10 is all you need if you can find the right dealer.

Then one evening, queuing for soup and a sandwich in the market place, another homeless person picked a fight. Mark, not afraid to defend himself, knocked the guy to the floor, collected his sandwich and went back to where he was planning to sleep that night and thought no more about it.

But a few nights later, they met again in the same soup run queue. The other chap pulled out a Stanley knife and slashed Mark across the face and arm. Police were called and the attacker is now in prison. Mark did not seek treatment straight away, but a few days later spent three nights in hospital having an operation on his damaged arm. The wound to his face was a clean cut, but has left him with a scar.

After this episode he was introduced to St Martins and slept in the 'sit-up room' at Bishopbridge House with others for the first few nights. Bishopbridge House provides 37 beds and the 'sit-up' room is used when all the single rooms are taken. You don't actually sit up at all, but sleep on one of four camp beds in this downstairs en-suite room. It was safer than the streets, where he was vulnerable to another attack as at that point, the guy who slashed his face and arm had not been caught by the police.

Then a single room became available and Mark stayed in the hostel for the next eight weeks. From here he moved on to a room in the Dibden Road hostel, and from here, after several months, to his own council flat, where he still lives today.

You could be forgiven for dismissing Mark as an ex-con with, at times, a bit of a drink habit. But you would be underestimating him if you did that. While in prison he trained to be a listener with Samaritans, supporting others who were suicidal or depressed. He had the opportunity with St Martins to volunteer a little too, helping other hostel tenants cope with life's challenges.

Just as the *Big Issue* helped him regain his financial independence, so too did St Martins act as a caring bridge between rough sleeping and taking on a council tenancy. He's not had an easy journey, and talks frankly about how, while he did drink, he never took drugs. Mark had a job interview the day after we met. He now works driving a forklift at a waste recycling facility. He's back on his feet and living proof that selling the *Big Issue* really can be a stepping stone back into employment.

Jim

To gain a greater insight into the work of the *Big Issue*, I met Jim Graver who is the magazine's Regional Manager for East Anglia. His office is at the ARC on Pottergate in Norwich. The ARC is run by the Salvation Army and a valuable drop-in centre for rough sleepers and other vulnerable people. It's a good place from which to distribute the magazine to vendors. It's where everyone who is homeless goes at some point.

Often on the road, as Jim is responsible for the *Big Issue* across the region, he called in to my home one day for a coffee as he was passing by. He'd been driving a while and didn't seem keen to sit down so we conducted our meeting standing up, which made taking notes difficult. But Jim is unafraid of publicity and I was able to find a number of online articles that served to remind me of what he had said.

Jim has worked for the *Big Issue* since 1995 and is something of a pioneer. When he joined, the magazine was in its infancy and as with most startups, the organisation was lean and everyone got involved with everything. What mattered was getting each issue published and on the streets.

The magazine launched in London and Jim had seen it on sale there. He thought it a good idea, so had little hesitation in applying when he saw that they were recruiting. Now more than 20 years on he has no regrets and has enjoyed the challenge of growing the brand in Eastern England. 'I was keen to find work which has in impact on the community around me,' he explained to me, 'and was impressed by the passion the founders had to make a real difference.'

The *Big Issue* has three clear goals. Firstly to provide opportunity for those who are disenfranchised to earn a living. Secondly, to break down the barriers that exist between homeless people and mainstream society. And thirdly, to provide what Jim described as an 'engaging and entertaining read'. Buying a copy requires you to speak with a vendor, which breaks the ice and is a whole lot better than begging, which for many is the only alternative.

While many assume that vendors are rough sleepers, most are living in a hostel or are vulnerably housed. Jim also told me about the Roma families, unable to access benefits or to find work, who very successfully take the *Big Issue* to market towns. This helps them survive and widens the distribution of the magazine.

We talked a little about the trend towards online publications. I was reassured to learn that the *Big Issue* remains popular in print format. An online version has been tested, with the vendor carrying a QR code that once scanned gives the buyer access to the latest edition online. Customer feedback was that people preferred to buy a copy they can hold in their hand. I'd already heard from Mark that good vendors quickly command customer loyalty. People will walk past three vendors to buy from their regular one each week.

I wondered why the *Big Issue* had not diversified to offer other products on the street. Jim explained that you could sell newspapers and periodicals on the street without first obtaining a Pedlar's Licence. This allows you to sell in the street, without having a permanent stall. *Big Issue* sellers are given a pitch, but because they're selling a magazine, they don't need to jump through hoops to obtain a licence.

I was also curious to know how city centre shopkeepers feel about having a *Big Issue* vendor working outside their shop. 'Most are fine,' Jim told me, 'and it's not unusual for cups of coffee and even sandwiches to be taken out.' For some, I learned, having a *Big Issue* vendor outside means having an early warning system: someone able to tip you off if a known shoplifter enters your premises. *Big Issue* sellers are usually pretty streetwise.

Jim's job is not always easy. Vendors need to be capable of a smile and polite conversation to sell to the public on the street. Some quickly develop their sales patter and others struggle. Success comes from hard work, commitment and an ability to invest your takings in buying more magazines. Not everyone accepts that.

Inevitably some will sell their copies, spend the money and then claim to have been robbed. Others will blame the magazine, the pitch they're given or anything but themselves for their inability to make it work. But as Jim told me, there are many people today who owe their return to the mainstream to the *Big Issue*.

Another downside to Jim's job is dealing with sudden deaths. Living rough can dramatically reduce life expectancy. Even when living in a hostel, the damage has often been done. It's not unusual to learn that a vendor has been found dead, or has died in hospital, often when still in their 40s.

Before he left, I asked Jim what he would like to say to those that read this book. This is what he said: 'It is my personal belief that eradicating homelessness completely will not happen in my lifetime, there will always be certain individuals that wish to live outside mainstream society while having the capacity to make their own decisions.

'The main things that would help is money for support services regarding housing, mental health services, adult social care, and also affordable housing, of which some needs to be supported housing.'

There is something of a Catch-22 situation when it comes to getting a job if you are homeless. You need an address to get a job, and a job to be able to afford to have an address. It's also pretty tough when you have a break in your employment history. Potential employers may be sympathetic if you've been on the streets, on drugs and maybe in prison, but when it comes to the crunch, most will make an excuse and turn you down.

Some employers, for example Timpsons, make a point of employing ex-offenders. People know that using Timpsons means you may be helping someone who has been in prison. Sandwich chain Pret A Manger has a Foundation that plans to provide accommodation for homeless people in London. They also plan to offer those they house work in one of their outlets.

Around the UK there are many social enterprises that choose to employ those on the margins of our society. A good example in Norwich was Café Britannia, which operated two cafes and a pub where they employ prisoners serving the final months of their sentences. Sadly at the time of writing, Café Britannia had closed. Many continued to work for the venture after they are released.

As social impact becomes more important as a way of differentiating your business in a competitive marketplace, the opportunity to provide employment to those returning from the horror of sleeping rough is very real. Everyone today would prefer to trade with a company that has a purpose beyond profit.

While it would be inappropriate to showcase your disadvantaged employees, knowing that people are recruited for their ability and attitude will surely make any business stand out. There are enough examples of now very successful people who have overcome addiction, poor mental health, homelessness and more, to show us all the importance of being truly inclusive employers.

5

A bed for the night

'What's money? A man is a success if he gets up
in the morning and goes to bed at night and in
between does what he wants to do.'
Bob Dylan

One thing I've taken for granted every day of my life is that I will have somewhere to sleep that night. I have a nice home and when travelling always know before setting off where I'll be staying that evening. Not every night has been comfortable, but I've always had a bed.

The memory of the very few bad nights I've experienced have stayed with me for years. I can remember staying one night in a particularly grotty French hotel. It looked fine from the outside, but the proprietor was strange, the room uncomfortable and the food, well, the food was well past its best. My wife and I found we were the only guests that night. We were not made to feel welcome. A fierce thunderstorm added to the sense of drama. But we had a bed.

For me, and I suspect for you, having somewhere safe,

clean and warm to sleep each night is taken for granted. Perhaps that's why when we are so disturbed when we see someone sleeping rough. It touches your sense of self, when you see a face poking out of a sleeping bag, on a sheet of cardboard in a shop doorway on a cold winter's morning. They look so vulnerable.

It's convenient to imagine that to be sleeping rough is a self-inflicted penalty for not pulling your weight in life. Is it really that difficult to get a job and place to live? Why has someone not got a family or friends they can stay with? What about the benefits system? Why is someone not claiming, or worse, are they squandering on drink or drugs the money the state has given them?

These thoughts are I guess what come to the minds of a group of lads on a night out who chance upon someone bedded down in a doorway. 'Hey, loser,' one shouts, with alcohol-fuelled bravado. The mumbled response does not appease, and so a poke with the foot, then a kick. Still he gets no response, so he unzips and pisses on the sleeping figure. His mates laugh, shoving him so his urine splashes the now wide awake rough sleeper's face. Then they walk away shouting into the night.

This happens. People who have slept rough tell me they've been kicked, pissed on and verbally abused. Not many years ago a rough sleeper was kicked to death in a Norwich city centre underpass. Life on the streets is undignified, brutal and often dangerous. Is Norwich a civilised city? I sometimes wonder.

Too few take the trouble to find out what has led someone to be sleeping rough. Nobody sets out to be homeless and for every person you see on the street, 50 more are likely to be sleeping in cars, or on a friend's floor, with no guarantee that they'll not be on the street themselves very soon. Statistically, only 2% of those without a permanent home sleep rough. Those we see represent the tip of a very large iceberg.

You'll remember that the *Big Issue* vendor Mark slept some nights in his brother's house and others in a tent which he pitched in a nearby park. This I've learned is pretty typical. You worry about jeopardising your benefits payments and putting too much strain on the household good enough to take you in. Relationship breakdown, redundancy, repossession and debt can quickly strip away all you've taken for granted and leave you confused, alone and with nowhere to sleep. Yes, it's scary.

Talking with Nick, one of the Trustees of St Martins, I'd learned about the rudimentary accommodation provided in a redundant church in the early days of the charity. Yes, there was little privacy and yes, you were turned out in the morning to fend for yourself. But at least you were safe from violence and theft. Few who slept there complained. All were grateful for the respite the place provided.

Another startling fact is that drugs and drink are easy to obtain on the streets of Norwich. They offer a temporary respite from the horror of the situation someone finds themselves in. Addiction can lead to crime, not through choice, but desperation. Even though it only costs £10 for enough crack cocaine to give you a decent high, this isn't cheap when you need to keep buying more.

Not surprisingly sleeping rough can hit your mental health too. Drink and drugs are for many a form of self-medication; a temporary escape from the horror of the life you find yourself living. Homelessness can be a consequence of poor mental health too. One in three of us will suffer poor mental health at some time in our lives. Depression and anxiety can distort our perceptions of reality, damage our relationships and make work impossible. It's another slippery slope.

We really do need to think, and perhaps ask a few questions, before writing off anyone we encounter sleeping in a doorway. In fact many I spoke to on my journey said that a polite 'hello', or 'how are you?' asked out of genuine compassion, could really lift their day. Surely we can all make time to say hello?

That draughty night shelter was replaced in 2002 by Bishopbridge House. I'd had a quick visit as part of my whistle stop tour of services. It was time to return and find out more about what happens here.

I arranged to meet Stacey, the manager, and two of her team. Bishopbridge House is where most people first encounter St Martins. Some people self-refer, or just turn up. Others are introduced by St Martins outreach workers, who tour the favourite spots chosen by those sleeping rough.

Stacey

Bishopbridge House is located in a part of the city with a lurid history. It sits just up the hill from the site of what was called Lollards pit, where heretics were burned at the stake in the 15th and 16th centuries. The Lollards were people who dared to challenge the supremacy of the church.

It seemed a somehow fitting location to provide support to those who today challenge our societal norms.

As you would expect, you can't just push the door and walk in. An intercom lets you explain why you're calling, and then from the reception area, there is another locked door to be let through to enter the staff area. With seating and information posters, it's rather like a doctors' waiting room.

Stacy came in to greet me, made coffee for us both and then we walked upstairs to her office on the first floor. I wasn't too sure which direction to take with the interviews, so started by asking what had brought Stacey to work in this challenging sector. Her answer surprised me. She had experienced homelessness herself and worked for St Martins to put her personal experience to good use.

Stacey first worked on Norwich Market, and then moved into care work. Her first experience of working at St Martins was as a locum support worker. She found this work more rewarding than working in care homes with sometimes very old people. Both client groups can be demanding, but she found she had more empathy with the homeless than the aged.

When the opportunity presented itself to join the team at St Martins, Stacey took it. She joined as a support worker, then became a team leader and now is Homeless Services Manager. She explained how working in this environment was both emotionally and at times physically challenging. It'd not something you do for the money, but for the satisfaction of helping vulnerable people.

Listening to Stacey as we drank our coffee, I sensed that here was someone who had found their niche in life. While clear boundaries are maintained between one's personal and professional life, having been vulnerably housed herself certainly helped her relate to those she found herself supporting.

Bishopbridge House is quite literally where many start their journey back from rough sleeping. People arrive vulnerable, sometimes afraid and often in a chaotic state. They've reached the lowest point in their lives, often quite unexpectedly, so Stacey and her team never quite know what to expect. Some will have very complex needs. Few are turned away; St Martins takes those other providers choose not to accept.

Understandably, within hours of arriving each person meets a support worker who agrees with them the help they need. Within the first three days a person will meet their support worker. No two people are the same, and only when someone is ready to be helped can they be supported. Stacey told me that some would stay for a few nights, then return to the streets, only to come back again a week or so later.

When people are ready to accept help, Stacey and her team can refer them to specialist services to help them overcome addiction or mental health problems. When someone has a criminal record and perhaps has only recently been released from prison, they are often on licence. This means they have to gain permission from their probation officer to travel, change where they live or take a job.

If their offence was violent or sexual then they may be subject to MAPPA, which stands for Multi Agency Public Protection Arrangements. Stacey represents St Martins at meetings with police, probation and other agencies to develop the risk management plans that are designed to keep both the public, and the ex-offender safe.

People can stay at Bishopgate House for up to two years, although most are ready to move on to more settled accommodation, usually a hostel within three months. There is always demand for beds at Bishopbridge House, so it's important for St Martins, as well as those staying there, to move on as soon as they are ready.

As you would expect, everyone who works at St Martins undergoes regular training. It's important to know how best to help those that come through the door. Being able to develop realistic fortnightly action plans with people takes some skill. Knowing what services they can be referred to requires having a good grasp of what is available. The support landscape is always changing.

Before I left Bishopbridge House, Stacey invited me to meet two of her team. This I was glad to do and was shown into the meeting room to wait. It was a chance to catch up on my emails; a temporary return to the comfort of my everyday life. Bishopbridge House is clean, tidy and the rooms surprisingly well appointed, but this is the front line in the quest to reduce rough sleeping. Just being here I found quite draining.

Alex

The door opened and Alex came in to the room. Like Stacey, he'd worked around homelessness for some time, joining the team from another hostel provider. As a senior support worker, he works a shift system, as the place is staffed 24 hours a day, 365 days a year. People can arrive at the door at any time of day or night and those already here can have difficult nights and need support.

Alex explained how many came here as a result of meeting one of his Pathways colleagues. I later went out with the outreach team, looking for rough sleepers. It was a sobering experience. It is a fact that people from a wide area tend to gravitate to a city centre when looking to sleep rough. That's why so many services for rough sleepers are concentrated in city centres.

It might appear romantic to sleep under a hedge in the countryside, but you won't find a soup kitchen, shower or place to dry a wet sleeping bag in a rural village. That's why homelessness is so visible in Norwich, as indeed it is in any city, especially London. You can sleep rough in the city and receive food, clothing and support. This is not the case in market towns or villages.

Within the first day or two of arrival, Alex, or more likely one of his Pathways colleagues, helps people complete a hostel application form. This piece of bureaucracy is important, as it allows St Martins to claim funding for the place they are providing. Most places are funded from housing benefits.

Not everyone is entitled to benefits and so some are unable to stay long at Bishopbridge House or anywhere else. It is estimated that at any one time, there are four or five people with 'no recourse to public funds'. Despite what many believe, you cannot arrive in the UK and claim benefits straight away.

One of Alex's jobs is to work with people to create and then support their fortnightly action plan. 'People have to want to change,' he explained, 'and some are too proud, or find it too difficult to ask for help. It can take a while for them to trust you enough to open up,' he added.

Before joining St Martins, Alex had worked for another provider of hostel accommodation. It's one to which people often move on to from Bishopbridge House. I think he prefers working here with people earlier in their journey. I guess you can see people make remarkable progress when staying here. I couldn't do what Alex does, but can see that it must be really rewarding work.

We chatted a bit about some of the other agencies clients are referred on to. Particularly interesting was the Norfolk Alcohol and Drug Behaviour Change Service, run by national charity Change, Grow, Live (CGL). Based near the railway station, they provide a free and confidential service for adults (including offenders), families, carers and other dealing with addiction.

Usefully CGL also provide a needle exchange and testing for blood-borne viruses such as HIV. Obviously taking drugs while on St Martins or any other provider's premises is not allowed. But it has to be accepted that some will be taking drugs elsewhere; helping them to do this more safely, while helping them to overcome the addiction, is both compassionate and practical.

I asked what happened when people were in secondary hostel accommodation. They're expected to stay there for no longer than two years. I know from mentoring an ex-offender in a bail hostel that people can become a little anxious as the two year mark is reached. But I also know that most will find a council flat when the time comes.

When the time comes to find a place of your own, Norwich is like most cities in that it bands applicants, with the most urgent being banded gold, then silver and bronze. Then each week the council lists places that are available.

Anyone seeking a place to rent can apply to the council to sign up, see what is available and bid. Qualification depends on a number of different factors, such as age, circumstances and how each case fits with housing act legislation. Housing Officers at City Hall meet applicants and talk each person through the process.

When able to bid for a place, an algorithm prioritises your bid according to your banding and how long you've been registered. When bidding closes, three are invited to view, and if the first chosen turns the pace down, then it is offered to the second and so on.

Curiosity prompted me to see if there was a housing options website for the local authority area within which I live. There was, so I suspect there's one for where you live too. It's interesting to pretend you're looking for a place and see what is available. Well, I found it interesting anyway!

A friend of mine in his early 60s found a flat in Norwich within weeks of signing up. I suspect it gives you a wider choice than a paper-based system ever could.

Alex had to get back to work, so left me in the meeting room where I was soon joined by his colleague Laura.

Laura

It was by chance that Laura came to work for St Martins. She'd been working nights for a care agency, and was offered a shift providing sickness cover at Bishopbridge House. She found the work and particularly the people interesting. A few months later she applied to join the team as a support worker, and soon, she will be moving to Dibden Road hostel. She's looking forward to that.

Talking with Laura gave me a real insight into the vulnerability of those who go there. I'd heard from others how prone rough sleepers are to become the victims of crime. Not just abuse or assault, but robbery too. It's just too easy to pick up someone's things when they're asleep in a doorway. Many wake up to find their mobile phone and any cash they had has disappeared.

There may be honour among thieves, but if your addiction is demanding attention, then stealing from a fellow rough sleeper is easier than shoplifting or begging. There's always someone who will buy what you've picked up without asking awkward questions.

That said, Laura told me people do forge strong friendships with other rough sleepers. It's good to have someone you can trust watching your back. While many have retained a bank account and so can quite easily access any benefits they're claiming, others do not use a bank and so have to carry cash. Some will feign friendship to borrow from someone they know has money in their pocket. It's hard to get repaid when you're all in the same boat; the excuses are easy to believe.

Just as we all tend to mix with people like ourselves, so too do rough sleepers. I for example regularly meet other writers, on Sundays I worship alongside other Quakers and socially, I mix with people with whom I have things in common.

We all do this and rough sleepers are no different. Laura told me how when someone comes to Bishopbridge House for the first time, they will usually bump into someone they already know. I'm always struck by the Dunbar number; that is the maximum number of people with whom we can form a relationship.

As Robin Dunbar found, instinctively our social circles rarely exceeds 150. That coincidentally is about the number of people at any one time sleeping on the streets or in a St Martins hostel. Together they form a community within a community.

Being a small community, rumours can spread quickly. Laura told me how some prefer to remain on the streets because they don't do drugs and believe Bishopbridge House to be something of a crack house. This of course is not true, although now and again, it is inevitable that a user will bring some in with them at night.

Also like any community there are those that stand out and those that prefer to keep a low profile. Laura repeated what Stacey had already told me, that some will come, stay a while then move back on to the streets, only to return again. You need great patience to work with these people.

But persistent kindness and non-judgemental encouragement to take the first steps eventually pays off. Stacey, Alex and Laura each made that point. There comes a moment in everyone's journey when hope slowly replaces despair and they begin to look forward not back. Those I guess are the moments that make working in this sector so worthwhile.

For a few however, that moment never really arrives. Their problems are simply so great that they need focused specialist help. So I left Bishopbridge House and set out to visit another St Martins hostel, this time Highwater House.

6

Bridges to cross

'It is not good to cross the bridge before you get to it.'
Judi Dench

Life can be rather like catching a train. Without the right ticket, you find a barrier stops you boarding and you miss the journey you had hoped to take. Then you find that because you are not in the place you hoped to be, you miss out on other things too. Sometimes circumstances seem to conspire against you. Life can appear far from fair.

As I hint at in the introduction to this book, I've had to overcome a few hurdles myself. One lasting consequence of those battles is a rather fragile sense of self. At times it can take very little to tip me into a deep depression. It can weeks then for me to regain my equilibrium. I know I'm far from alone in that respect.

I take some comfort from Newton's Third Law, which states that for every action, there is an equal and opposite reaction. In other words, every dark spell in my life is matched by a similar period of startling clarity and sensitivity. I think I need this to be effective as a writer.

It's why so many creative people thorough the ages have struggled with their mental health. It perhaps explains why painter Vincent Van Gogh, composer Otto Mahler and writer Ernest Hemingway all took their own lives. Is talent the consequence of an inner conflict, or vice versa? That is open for debate.

It would be wrong to assume that all rough sleepers have problems with their mental health. Some are certainly talented, as some of the art I saw on my travels illustrated. It would also be wrong to assume that they are all hopelessly addicted to drink or drugs.

To believe these negative things is to reinforce the damaging stereotypes society conveniently projects onto those we encounter living on the street. Catching sight of someone huddled in a door way with a sleeping bag and some sheets of cardboard provides an unwelcome reminder of the fragility of our lives.

But like any other community of people, every rough sleeper is unique with hopes, fears, ambitions and challenges. Our challenge is to take the trouble to listen to those ambitions and understand those fears. Above all else, those living on the streets are people, just like you and me.

It is, however, fair to say that homelessness can be something you bounce back from fairly quickly, or it can hit you really hard. Many people working to address the issue whom I spoke to as I researched this book talked of having been homeless and even rough sleeping for a period in their past. It's natural to want to put your own personal experience to good use. That's why many with lived experience work in this field.

For a few however, the experience can be truly devastating

and push them into a place from where it is very, very hard to return. It was my desire to understand the help available for this group that took me to Highwater House, just off the inner ring road in Norwich.

Highwater House is a hostel that caters for the some of the most troubled people who find themselves homeless. Technically, it is a care home for people recovering from addiction or mental health problems. In reality it is place you can be sure of a welcome when everywhere else has turned you away.

Sleeping rough is traumatic for anyone, but for some it destroys their sense of self-worth and they sink into a pit of despair. Drink or drugs provide some respite, but this of course simply pushes you further away from the society from which you have fallen. It is no wonder that mental health problems are often a consequence of sleeping rough.

For some, mental health problems are the reason they became homeless in the first place. I met people who had become ill, got in a muddle with their rent and not been able to ask for help. Only when living on the street were they able to accept the hand of friendship extended by one of St Martins' outreach team. I'm sure that other agencies reach out too, but St Martins was the charity I learned most about. It's also the charity you have supported by buying a copy of this book.

To work at Highwater House takes a special sort of person. You need the resilience to cope with the highs and lows your service users experience. You need to be able to accept that for some who come here, the concepts of generosity and love are alien. They can take weeks to trust those here to support them. They can struggle to accept the help that is offered and sometimes they can kick off and be violent, because the stress of their situation has become simply unbearable.

Managing this 22 bed unit is Angela. I visited Highwater to talk with her and gain an insight into how this place has become so skilled at turning round severely damaged lives. When I visited, they'd just been rated outstanding by the Care Quality Commission. That is no small achievement for a place where the unpredictable is something that happens nearly every day. To compare it with a cosy old folks' home, where losing your false teeth is considered a crisis, Highwater House is something quite different.

Yes it got to me. Yes visiting this place moved me and I make no apology for my enthusiasm for what I saw here. But let me return to objectivity and tell you about my conversation with Angela.

Angela

Like so many I've met in this sector, Angela did not set out to work with homeless people. But joining the team to provide maternity cover, she found the work rewarding although challenging and has been with the organisation for 20 years.

Highwater House only opened in 2008. Before that the building was a hostel with many more beds, catering for people moving on from the night shelter. It was busy then, but there was not space or time to provide the level of care made possible by the restructuring of the building into what it is today.

I asked what made it different today. 'We now cater for

people who have high needs,' Angela explained, 'and can help people with personal care, for example bathing, and give them their medication.' She went on to explain that some people were simply not able to look after themselves, at least not until they'd been here some while.

'You have to understand,' she said, 'that people may have never had a positive relationship with anyone in their life. People find it hard to believe we provide three meals a day, as well as meals at other times if that's what someone wants.' She told me that in the early days, it is not unusual for a resident to put food in their pockets at the counter, because they simply cannot believe that the next meal will be there in a few hours' time.

While many staying here have mental health problems, therapy is not part of the package. The place was described to me as a 'psychologically informed environment', where everything is geared to provide space within which each resident can develop and grow. The local GP practice I was told provides excellent support, coming out to see those unable to get to the surgery.

Obviously people are not allowed to take drugs here, although they may well return when under the influence. They can however drink, because if not, some would drink by the nearby river. It's not unknown for people to fall in and drown, trapped against the downstream weir.

Angela told me that some are totally overwhelmed when they arrive to find a single, en suite room, to which they have their own key. For some, she told me, it had been years since they'd slept in a bed or used a toilet. People when they arrive may have no spare clothes, not have seen a doctor for years and be malnourished and underweight.

Not surprisingly, the priority in the early days is to get them cleaned up, properly clothed and in front of the GP for a medical. Once people have food in their tummy, clean clothes and have had a few nights' good sleep, they begin to open up. 'Often,' Angela said, 'we are the first people they have ever told about the traumas that have led to them needing our support.'

Not everyone manages to move on from Highwater House. Some remain here for years, and others sadly come to the end of their lives here. The team are not specialists in providing palliative care; but they are more than willing to make it possible for people to die here, if that is their wish. Remember that life on the streets is short; the risk of dying in your 40s simply comes from the harshness of a life sleeping rough. Drink, drugs and poor diet don't help. Organ failure is how life ends for many.

As you might imagine, working here can be hard. Angela keeps a watchful eye on her team for signs of stress. Sometimes somebody has to be tactfully asked to take some time out. Sometimes you can be overwhelmed by it all. For example every now and then a resident has to be sectioned and admitted to the local mental health hospital. It can take more than 24 hours from asking for help, to that help arriving. Staff cannot leave someone alone if they're having a psychotic episode. Going home at the end of your shift, at times, just might not happen.

That said, Angela was proud of the fact that she has a low turnover of staff and little time lost due to sickness. That perhaps is one reason why this place received such a positive CQC inspection report.

Again I was told that nobody chooses to be homeless, or

to have a mental health problem, or can really be blamed for self-medicating with drink or drugs. After all, both are readily available and most people drink; some just drink more than others. I was reminded of my late father, who drank to excess in his own struggle with the demons that haunted him. He lost the battle and died an alcoholic in his mid-50s.

What became apparent chatting with Angela was that this place becomes someone's home, and those living here, their family. I was worried that creating dependence meant people were reluctant to move on. Angela told me it's actually not like that; just as children grow up and leave home, so too do residents here become more confident and, in time, eager to move on to a place of their own.

I started this chapter by explaining how I feel that Newton's Third Law can apply to life. Just as Highwater House supports those with severe problems, it is no coincidence that right next door, is Under 1 Roof, a St Martins training and development centre. Here those who are homeless or vulnerable can develop new skills that can help them return to living independently.

In Norwich, those furthest from getting a home of their own and a job are housed next door to the place where others are helped to do just that. It might be me, but I find this juxtaposition fascinating. These two services bracket the spectrum of support offered to those who are homeless.

Phil

Under 1 Roof started out as a service to help those using St Martins' services become work-ready. If you've been out of work and homeless, you often need help building your confidence and updating your computer skills to get a job. The range of activities on offer can appear confusing at first, so I asked Phillip who manages the service to talk me through what happens here.

By now I was not surprised to learn that as with so many I met, Phil has first-hand experience of homelessness. Perhaps understandably, he did not want to talk about this. When we met he was planning to have some work done to the conservatory at his home. That in itself told me all I needed to know. Here is a man who may have experienced real hardship, but has bounced back and is probably all the stronger for the experience.

To take a course here you have to join and be a member. Member is a far nicer term than service user. Here it's an indication of the respect shown to those that use this place. I'm a member of my local gym. The only difference at Under 1 Roof is that members don't have to pay. They just have to commit to turning up and taking part.

Phil described managing Under 1 Roof as 'spinning plates'. There is never a dull moment and every day can bring unexpected challenges. It's the nature of the membership here that some will be struggling and others pushing ahead. Members can drop in to use a computer at any time, as well as join one of the courses that are always running. Phil talked me through what was on offer when I visited.

Listening to him I soon grasped the fact that everything on offer here is geared to help the member improve their life. So the 'Building Better Habits' programme, which runs on two afternoons over a week, helps you feel better about yourself. Members can learn techniques for managing anger, coping with negative thoughts and so build their self-esteem.

Once the world starts to look brighter, you might join a keep fit class, which is great for your wellbeing. It's both social and a chance to release some endorphins, which will make you feel better about yourself too. Over four consecutive Fridays you can also join a 'Joy of Food' programme that gives you the opportunity to both prepare and eat food. On completion you receive a recipe book, ready for when you get a place of your own.

Phil told me how sometimes people have become homeless because they could not maintain a tenancy. As he pointed out, if you've lived most of your life in an institution you won't necessarily know the things most of us take for granted. There are he explained, people who grow up in care, then spend time in the armed forces, or perhaps prison, and so when given the keys to a home of their own, really struggle to cope.

Until recently the local council offered a four-session tenancy course. At Under 1 Roof the course is longer, running over eight weeks and covering all you need to know and more.

While the council course covers managing money and your responsibilities as a tenant, Under 1 Roof also includes sessions on heath, hygiene and nutrition. It's good to learn to look after yourself, as well as your flat.

Meeting Phil was also interesting because he shattered one or two assumptions even I was still making about homeless people. 'Quite a few rough sleepers have jobs,' he explained, 'usually in a factory and often through an agency.' I suspect that many more take temporary work; it's hard to plan ahead when you have nowhere to live.

Thinking about it, I could see how, providing you had a bike and looked fairly presentable, you could become a delivery rider without anyone knowing you were actually sleeping rough. And of course the problem with zero hours contracts was that you never knew how much you were going to earn. It only goes to show that you really cannot ever make an assumption about anybody.

Under 1 Roof offer a range of arts courses too. If you've lived an interesting life, as of course most members have, then it's good to share your experience through music, art or writing. 'You'd be surprised how good some of the art produced here is,' Phil told me. He had been so struck by one member's design he has had it tattooed onto his arm. That surely is the ultimate accolade for any artist?

Phil himself is a musician and, he said, confident on a sound mixing desk. Perhaps this is one reason why on the Under 1 Roof website you can buy a compilation CD titled Under 1 Riff, including recordings by in-house band The Undies. Fans can also buy T-shirts, with all profits going to support the work of Under 1 Roof.

When I arrived, Phil had explained how members were free to come in at any time and use the computers. This of course is important, as it allows them to access their emails, access online banking and catch up with friends on social media. Keen to see if there were any downsides to Under 1 Roof, I asked if they ever had problems with drink, drugs or violence.

His answer reassured me. Drink and drugs are not allowed on the premises, but every now and then someone will kick off and vent their anger at life on whatever comes to hand. 'It's because they feel safe here,' Phil explained. 'We are their club, and not like the Job Centre which some find daunting.' (Although as I'd found earlier, the staff and systems at the DWP are far more user friendly than even I had realised.)

'In my years here,' Phil said, 'I've only had to permanently ban one person, because there was a high risk he would be violent and disruptive.' Others are sometimes banned for as little as 24 hours or in rare cases, a month for bad behaviour. We all have off days and being a member of Under 1 Roof is no different to belonging to any other network. We all at times feel the urge to kick the cat, metaphorically speaking of course.

It was time to let Phil get back to his busy day. I needed to reflect on what motivated people to work in what at times can be an emotionally challenging sector. Some, as I was finding, are motivated by personal experience. Others I know are motivated by their faith. But before we move on to explore that, let me introduce one more member of the St Martins team with you.

Jim

Highwater House and Under 1 Roof to me represent two extreme points of the journey back from rough sleeping and homelessness. One supports those wrestling with particularly severe challenges. The other helps people develop and achieve new goals.

But not everybody that benefits from the St Martins services uses these two. Many quite quickly move into a supported hostel, or share house, where they can stay for a couple of years. Usually from here they secure their own tenancy, find work and rejoin mainstream society.

Jim manages one of these hostels and one afternoon I visited for a cup of coffee and a chat. With a small team to support him, Jim runs the place in a friendly but firm way. He finds it easy to empathise with his residents as he too, has experience of homelessness.

He knows all the tricks people sometimes play. He didn't say, but perhaps has used a few of them himself. He has been a drug user as well as a drinker, and knows that when hooked, people can be really quite creative to fund their next fix. Some for example, when placed in a guest house by the council, will persuade the proprietor to refund them some of the money that's been paid for their room, then sleep rough and spend the money on drugs.

Equally, knowing where to find free food in the city means that more of one's benefits payment can be spent on drugs. This must be particularly hard, if not impossible to police. These facts serve as reminders that to move on from homelessness, you have to want to change. Each and every one of us has choice about how we live, even those with nowhere to live.

Jim has worked at Dibden Road for a long time. In fact he was employed there by the housing association that used to run the place, then transferred to St Martins when they took over the hostel. The building still belongs to the housing association, with which St Martins enjoy an excellent working relationship.

Despite having live experience, Jim is careful to maintain professional boundaries. He makes no secret that he has taken drugs and been in prison, but while this makes empathy easy, his personal life is clearly none of the residents' business.

In this line of work, boundaries also have to be drawn when it comes to drugs. Many residents will be users, but there is a zero tolerance approach to bringing drugs into the hostel. I was reminded of the widely reported case in Cambridge around 20 years ago. Here two hostel workers were jailed for 'knowingly permitting' drugs to be peddled at the hostel.

Turning a blind eye is something you simply cannot afford to do. In the Cambridge case, one received a five year sentence and the other four years. These sentences were particularly harsh, as any sentence over four years is never spent. In other words, you have to disclose it whenever you apply for a job for the rest of your life.

So working at a hostel for homeless people comes with its risks, but for Jim, it's worthwhile because you are able to help people turn their lives around. 'I just love this job,' he told me, 'and seeing someone leave because they now have a place of their own, and perhaps a job, is what makes me get out of bed in the morning, even when I know the day will be tough.'

I asked Jim what he thought people reading this book could do to help. 'By all means give people food, or maybe money,' he suggested, 'but most of all give them your time, either by stopping to speak with someone on the street, or by volunteering with one of the homelessness organisations in your city.'

I guess I would add to that the thought that it's easy to overthink helping someone who is clearly distressed and in a fix. Yes, they might spend the money you give them on drugs, so if you choose to give it to a charity instead, tell them that this is why you are turning them down. Don't just walk away.

7

Faith in humanity

*'The first question which the priest and the Levite asked was:
"If I stop to help this man, what will happen to me?" But …
the good Samaritan reversed the question: "If I do not
stop to help this man, what will happen to him?"'*
Martin Luther King

Religion has been at the heart of civilisation for millennia. It has been the cause of wars, prejudice and oppression. It has also been a tremendous force for good, inspiring millions to act for the common good, rather than focusing purely on their own wants and needs.

A recent (2017–18) British Museum exhibition illustrated how the 6,000 religions in the world today have led to ancient temples being erected, fine paintings created and beautiful music composed. People have always been inspired by a belief in something greater than themselves.

I am a Quaker, a member of the Religious Society of Friends that grew out of the newly formed Church of England in the 1640s, though my view is that no religion is more worthy of support than any other. We are all equal in the world, and nobody has the right to tell someone else that the religion they've chosen to follow is anything but the right one for them. What matters is that we believe something.

But I would be a fool not to acknowledge that Western Europe has a rich Christian tradition. Norwich, my local city, has 31 surviving mediaeval churches, most still used for the purpose for which they were built. St Martins – as in the homelessness charity– was founded by the Dean of Norwich Cathedral. Its first night shelter was situated in a redundant mediaeval church on Barrack Street, and in 1976 this moved to another one on the city's Oak Street, St Martin at Oak, from which it took its name. Need I say more?

I can also say that had I not been a Quaker, I would not have had the experiences that led me to write this book. Friends (Quakers refer to each other as Friend) were concerned about rough sleeping and unsure how best to help. You can feel powerless if you want to do something but are unsure how best to make a difference. So I set out to find out and realised that writing a book would help people better understand the issue.

It was inevitably that on this journey I would meet people who felt very strongly that God had played a significant part in their life. Indeed it's been suggested that God had a hand in my decision to write this book. In this chapter I talk with three people. One has experienced homelessness and his religion he told me saved him.

Another felt called by God to do some frankly amazing things to help those on the streets over several decades.

The third became a Christian in his teens, worked in the homelessness sector, went to prison, almost became a rough sleeper and is now an ordained minister and writer, working in prison education.

Meeting each one of them I found deeply moving. Their confidence that God had played a major part in their lives was compelling and frankly inspiring. But equally I understand that you might find that religious conviction disturbing. What is more important than why, is simply that they each did what they did.

Fred

Fred did not have a happy childhood. Raised in a family of Jehovah's Witnesses, he rebelled and discovered cannabis at the age of 14. He found the comfort in drugs that he had not found at home and over the next few years, his habit developed. He married at 18 and had a daughter, but the marriage did not last.

Over the next few years, Fred used amphetamines and then heroin. He remarried and had three more children, but his addiction remained the main focus of his waking hours. He had a succession of jobs, none of which lasted very long. Life became a maelstrom, tossing him around as he strove to earn enough to support his family and feed his habit.

After 10 years of marriage his wife decided that she had endured enough. Fred now found himself with nowhere to live. Without a job, crime became the only way he could buy the drugs his body now craved. One day, pursued by the police, he fell several storeys from a window and broke his back. He avoided arrest, was found and taken to hospital where he gave a false name to avoid detection.

After a week the police caught up with him and he was arrested in hospital. A prison sentence followed, which gave him the opportunity to come off drugs. But as he explained, 'I found a dealer and bought heroin on the day I was released. I no longer cared if I lived or died. I had reached the bottom.'

While serving a subsequent prison sentence Fred underwent the 12 step Alcoholics Anonymous therapeutic process to break his addiction. Looking this up, I was surprised to see that God features strongly in three steps. The second step is to 'Come to believe that a Power greater than ourselves could restore us to sanity,' and the third, is to 'make a decision to turn our will and our lives over to the care of God as we understand Him'.In the final step of the 12, the former addict commits to carry the message to others suffering at the hands of their own addiction. I can now understand why others I know who have gone through this process have become so evangelical about it.

Fred however had the opportunity to remember the teachings and faith in God he had been brought up with. He was visited by a Jehovah's Witness chaplain, who knew of his upbringing and made time to listen. Over a period, they studied the Bible together and as Fred's faith returned, so too did his appetite for life. He had, he told me, become quite depressed while in prison. With the chaplain's help he turned a corner and started to make plans for the future.

For the final year of his sentence, Fred moved to Britannia House, an open unit, outside the walls of Norwich Prison. From here he was able to get a job and attend a local congregation of Jehovah's Witnesses. Now he had the opportunity to drink and use drugs, but no longer had the urge.

Having a job helped Fred secure a council flat when he was finally released from prison. He trained as an addiction counsellor and often visited people who had said they were struggling with drink or drugs when visited by a Jehovah's Witness. He also started working in a hostel, where others recovering from addiction, and also homeless, are accommodated.

'It helps enormously that I have been where they are,' Fred explained, 'because when I suggest that life will get better once you stop using, people are more inclined to believe me.' Fred's own experience of homelessness, one he shares with so many other people working in the sector, no doubt helps the service user and this in turn, I suspect, strengthens his own recovery.

Fred's story has something of a happy ending. Now happily married to a childhood sweetheart, he is once more in touch with his children. His son, he said, had started taking cannabis and was in danger of following in his father's footsteps. He has been able to help his son rekindle his own faith, which has led to him getting a good job and averting the disastrous episodes that Fred has lived through.

I asked Fred what he would like to say to you, reading this book. He said that 'we have to encourage people to take control of their futures'. This cannot be easy if depressed, addicted and homeless, but he added 'we can only help people if they decide to help themselves'.

We then touched on the fact that sometimes as many as

80 people line up for free food in the city centre each night. 'Those who go to the Haymarket for food are desperate needy people,' Fred explained, 'and if we make it too easy for people, they won't face up to their situation.'

That's not to say that Fred thinks feeding homeless people is wrong, but that for some, it can put off their decision to seek help to deal with their problems. A number of groups feed people in the Haymarket and you can get food there every night of the year. Apart from seeing people sitting or sleeping in shop doorways, this is perhaps one of the most visible signs of rough sleeping in the city. I suspect it's the same in other cities too.

I had met Fred at the hostel where he works. When I'd arrived, one of the residents had agreed to talk with me, but when the time came, he'd gone out. People coming back from homelessness often find it difficult to fit in with other people's agendas. They've spent too long having to single-mindedly focus on their survival, to worry too much about what others might expect of them.

A few days later, with my visit to the hostel still in my mind, I visited the Norwich Salvation Army Citadel. This imposing city centre building had long intrigued me and I arranged to meet Barry there. Each Sunday I drive past the building on my way to Quaker Meeting. I always hope to find a place to park on the street, but every space is already taken when I pass. There are often more than 200 people at the Sunday Salvation Army service. I always have to park elsewhere.

Barry

Barry coordinates the Salvation Army soup run. When he first came to Norwich and got involved, the soup run was just that: visiting rough sleepers where they slept, to offer hot soup and sandwiches. For the past few years, it has operated from a stall on the city's Haymarket, next to the marketplace and close to City Hall.

'Until seven years ago the Salvation Army alone provided this service,' Barry told me, 'but now thankfully there are other groups.' Barry organises the rota so that effort is not duplicated. Other groups include the People's Picnic, the Norwich Soup Movement and Norwich Empathy Action and Time (EAT). Another group, Food and Beverage Buggies, take food, clothing and bedding out to rough sleepers who choose not to use the Haymarket feeding station.

Another group, Food Cycle, use the Quaker Meeting house to prepare and serve a Friday evening meal using surplus food donated by retailers and others. All of these groups are non-judgemental, volunteer-run and committed to helping people in need, regardless of whether they are homeless or not.

I must confess to having started this journey with some scepticism towards these grassroots movements that spring up and feed people on the street. But as my understanding of homelessness has increased, I have nothing but respect for those that step in and do something positive. People who are vulnerable and alone need others to take an interest in their plight and offer friendly support. I suspect Barry has a far from easy task coordinating these different groups' activity.

Barry bought me a coffee in the Citadel's café and we adjourned to a quiet room to talk. A modest man, who claims no credit for the work he has done over the years, Barry refers to those fed on the Haymarket as his friends and guests. He told me about how he came to be in Norwich and so involved with supporting rough sleepers. As with Fred, God had a hand in Barry's journey.

From an early age, Barry had been fascinated by numbers. Perhaps unusually, he wanted to be an accountant when he grew up, which he did. As a teenager he also wanted to help with youth work, and this, and an interest in motor bikes, led to Barry and a group of friends joining a Salvation Army youth club in his home town.

This revitalised the flagging youth club and gave it an unusual bias towards bikers; not a group you readily associate with the Salvation Army. Barry told me that while he was keen on the youth club, he felt no urge to attend Salvation Army services. Religion did not play a part in his life. That is, until a few years later.

'I was walking home one day and God spoke to me,' Barry explained, 'telling me that I should become a Salvation Army officer.' He quickly dismissed the thought as he by then had his own accountancy practice. Life was busy enough, he thought, without adding religion to his already hectic schedule.

But as he told me, God was not prepared to take no for an answer and so one day he visited his local Citadel and told the surprised Salvationists he met that 'God wants me to become a Salvation Army officer'. They gently explained that first he had to become a member, and then he could perhaps train to become an officer. This he later did.

The Norwich Salvation Army Citadel was built in 1898 and in 1974 extended, with the purchase of the former Mortimer's Hotel. In the 1990s the adjacent Conservative Club was purchased as part of a million pound project to improve the Citadel and provide more space for outreach activities.

This rapid expansion and the need to complete the fundraising, so that the new building could be converted, was what brought Barry to Norwich. He was by then an officer and trained accountant, so one of few with the financial skills, faith and determination to take on this task. He successfully led the fundraising campaign, oversaw the work and for a number of years, was the lead Minister at the Citadel.

Now happily retired, although when we met Barry's wife was not enjoying good health, I wondered why he still volunteered to lead the soup run. After all, it is stressful work and surely, we all reach an age when a good book and a blazing fire is preferable to standing out in the cold with the homeless.

But Barry is not one to put his own comforts ahead of those of others. He told me how a number of years ago he had been invited to speak to a Salvation Army audience in South Africa. He wanted to see what he called 'real life' on his visit, and so asked to be accommodated in Soweto, one of the townships.

This caused a few eyebrows to be raised, but Barry was determined. Of the Soweto population of more than a million, fewer than 1,000 are white. With apartheid still fresh in people's memories, people were surprised that Barry should choose to stay in a township. The township had a vibrant Salvation Army citadel and Barry naturally wanted to visit. He told me that he found the experience powerful. He saw first-hand the extreme poverty so common in Africa and returned to the UK with renewed determination to do what he could for homeless people, both at home and abroad.

Being an officer in the Salvation Army is no easy ride. Yes, you are paid a modest salary and often provided with a place to live, but equally you are expected to engage with those most in our society choose to ignore. The Salvation Army have a reputation for quietly and efficiently getting involved with all kinds of humanitarian work.

In Norwich, the Salvation Army also run a drop-in centre called the ARC. It is set aside for the exclusive use of rough sleepers for the first hour of each day. People can have some breakfast, take a shower and do their laundry here. It is staffed by members of the Pathways team, and is also where the local *Big Issue* office is located.

The Salvation Army is perhaps one of the most effective movements for social change in the world today. While modest, Barry has devoted most of his life to making a difference, both spiritually as a church leader, but also practically, at the front line of the fight against poverty, supporting those who sleep rough. After our conversation, Barry showed me round the citadel. Both the man and the building impressed me hugely.

It is very easy to be critical of the support offered to those who become homeless. As I've said already, those we encounter sleeping rough represent perhaps just one in 50 of those at risk. In part to show you how well the system can work, and in part because I want to include someone whose journey has impressed me, let me introduce you to my friend Mark.

Mark

I got to know Mark because he often attends the Quaker Meeting of which I am a member. Quaker Meetings attract people from a broad spectrum of faith background. And Mark is far from the only ordained minister who finds solace in the stillness of Quaker worship. You will find Mark's story interesting because it illustrates how someone homeless can be successfully supported into their own flat.

Mark was released from prison in spring 2018. He had been given a life sentence at the age of 25 for 13 arson attacks on property. 'Luckily nobody got hurt,' he told me. 'Then one day the penny dropped, I knew what I had done was wrong, so I walked into a police station and handed myself in,' he added.

A trained chef, he was studying at Bible College with a view to ordination. He'd been a Christian since he was in his teens, and at the time of his arrest was working in London, feeding homeless people in a church run hostel. He continued his studies while in prison, where he found his faith helped him, and others who confided in him, sharing their hopes, fears and anxieties.

Mark was diagnosed as bipolar and spent three of his 10 years in prison at HMP Grendon, a unique prison in that a therapeutic programme sits at the core of the establishment. The relationship between staff and prisoners here is very different to that in a mainstream prison. An ongoing therapeutic dialogue helps prisoners to understand and change their behaviour. Grendon helps prisoners develop more positive relationships, to change how they relate to others and to reduce their risk of reoffending.

In Mark's case this certainly worked, and he completed his sentence at HMP Sudbury in Derbyshire. His then partner had a smallholding in Norfolk and Mark settled to a life of growing vegetables and rearing pigs. It was a happy time, but the relationship ended and Mark, still on licence, moved to a probation hostel.

It was while here that what he describes as a 'silly argument over football' led to him being recalled to prison, where he served a further four years at HMP Wayland. As his release date neared, Mark made contact with The House of Genesis, a Christian charity that runs two hostels in Norwich. They offered him a room and from here, he secured a place of his own.

While in prison Mark started an Open University degree course in English Literature and Creative Writing. Now halfway through, he writes crime fiction, poems and is a newspaper columnist. Mark has a job as Broadcast Coordinator for Wayout TV, a company producing educational programmes that are broadcast to prisoners in their cells.

Mark's story shows how, with somewhere to go when you leave prison and a positive outlook, you can use your experience to take your career in a new direction. His Christian faith helped him and perhaps that helped him secure a hostel place with a Christian organisation when he was released.

But Mark also returned to education while behind bars, filling his time with his studies, rather than languishing in despair, as he could so easily have done. He must have revisited many times in his mind the episode that led to his return to prison for an additional four years.

Neither drugs nor drink was mentioned when Mark and I spoke. I suspect that his faith gave him hope and strength, in situations where others sought sanctuary in drugs. He had the opportunity to take drugs in prison, as of course we all read in the press that drugs do find their way into prison.

What became clear to me writing this chapter was that the three people I met had all felt that God had chosen the road they were going to travel. Fred and Mark had of course had troubled early lives that had led them to offend and service prison sentences. But Barry had been happy running his own successful accountancy practice until he was called into service with the Salvation Army.

Are there lessons here for the rest of us I wonder? Clearly religion has a place in our society and, for those I met here, it has given them the stability and focus to lead positive change, both in their own lives and those of the people they work with. Indeed this has also been to some extent my own experience. Were I not a Quaker I would not have written this book.

It would be foolish to suggest that it is a lack of faith that prompts people to abuse, attack or simply ignore the homeless person they encounter on the street. But to overlook the fact that people who are living rough are no different to you or me, is to accept the thin end of a very unpleasant wedge. Racism and homophobia are similar human traits that can lead to prejudice and even violence.

My sense is that the more we legislate to encourage

equality and prevent discrimination, the more we somehow highlight difference, with prejudice and fear the result. People need to become more tolerant of those living differently to themselves. Let's now move on and see how others have re-built their lives after a spell of sleeping rough.

8

Are you ready for old age?

*'Old age is like a plane flying through a storm.
Once you're aboard, there's nothing you can do.'*
Golda Meir

Old age is something we all face and should come as no surprise. We first see it in our grandparents, who grow old and then die, usually when we are young adults. In my 30s, when my last surviving grandparent died, I could not imagine what it would be like to become old, infirm and dependent on others. I quickly put such thoughts to one side and pressed ahead with my busy life.

When our parents die, we are usually in late middle age, and so beginning to feel the effects of wear and tear. We are by then painfully aware that what we are seeing our parents go through is what awaits us. Late middle age is often a time of bucket lists and finally making time to fulfil long held ambitions. I for example bought a piano when I reached 60 and started taking lessons.

But even in our 60s, we can ignore the fact that in 20 years' time we will be old ourselves. I read a press article recently that suggested that 2044 would see the UK death rate peak, before slowly declining. I will be 89 years old in 2044. None of my family has lived beyond that age. I very much doubt I will live to see 2045.

For people who habitually find themselves living rough, old age is not something they have to worry about. Life expectancy for a man living rough is just 44. For women, it's just 42, so even lower. Some, as you would expect, freeze to death, but many more succumb to infection.

Alarmingly, you are 17 times more likely to die a violent death if you live on the street than if you spend each night safely tucked up in bed in your own home. With life on the streets so bleak and brutal, it's perhaps no surprise that rough sleepers are nine times more likely to kill themselves than the rest of us.

It's obvious I guess that if you're living rough, perhaps moving from place to place in search of food and relative safety, you're unlikely to visit your GP. In fact you most likely won't have a GP. Your first consultation with a doctor is likely to be as you're wheeled out of an ambulance into the accident and emergency department of your local hospital.

In Norwich we have City Reach, a walk-in GP service for those who don't have a regular GP and don't feel comfortable visiting a practice surgery. Their website says that they cater for 'people who are homeless, or those at risk of being homeless, sex workers, prisoners and ex-offenders, substance mis-users, travellers and asylum seekers'.

The list probably contains all the groups of people you would prefer not to bump into at your local GP surgery. But they are all people with a story to tell. Few I suspect, apart perhaps from travellers, set out to live the way of life that brings them through the door of City Reach. Working there must be an emotional rollercoaster. I guess the staff have to maintain a calm, professional distance from those who walk through the door.

I set out to find out what happened to rough sleepers when they get old. Not all die in their 40s, but you rarely see an old man sitting in a shop doorway. 'Where do they all go?' I asked myself. Well, I'd started my whirlwind tour of St Martins services at Webster Court, a 33-bed sheltered housing scheme that caters for people with a history of substance abuse, poor mental health, or both. The home sits in a pleasantly tree-lined corner of Norwich, at the end of a cul-de-sac. It's one of those parts of Norwich you never see unless to visit someone who lives there.

Joy

My ring on the doorbell was answered by Joy, the manager at Webster Court. Over a coffee she told me a little about the place. The home opened in 2015, thanks to a £250,000 grant from the County Council and three legacies totalling £210,000. A further £240,000 was raised to enable the £700,000 refurbishment of the building to take place.

Joy clearly loves her job. She's been with St Martins for years, having previously managed a hostel on Carrow Hill. 'The people who live here did not set out to become homeless,' she explained, 'but here they have a place they can call their home.' You have to be aged over 50 to live here, but once there, can stay for the rest of your life.

I knew from my earlier tour that the accommodation comprised one bedroomed flats, some with shared kitchen but all with their own front door. For some, this was the first time they had been able to call anywhere home.

This is not one of those old folks' homes where everyone comes together to eat at fixed times. People here shop for food, prepare their meals and so eat what and when it suits them. After all, this is their home. I guess it's important that this place is nothing like an institution. Many who live here will have been raised in children's homes or served prison sentences. They deserve the freedom they enjoy here.

Of course residents here can come and go as they please. I on the other hand as a visitor had to ring a bell and announce who I was over an intercom. I guess you can't just let anyone in without first knowing why they were there.

Joy explained how people's places here were funded by the benefits system. This meant they were free, for perhaps the first time, of financial worry. The benefits system also made sure they had money for food and clothing. And perhaps importantly, friendly advice was never far away if anyone was worried about making ends meet.

Of course as people grow older, their health and mobility can decline. Funding for additional care is sought when residents need it. I got the sense, though, that whatever was funded was topped up by a caring staff, willing wherever possible to go beyond what was expected. It's human nature to want to help maintain dignity and control as you grow old and become frail.

It seemed nice that you could come here in your 50s, and stay for the rest of your life, with the comfort of being in familiar surroundings. In fact while here, I met someone who hoped to do just that.

Rita

Joy took my up a flight of stairs to the corridor along which Rita's flat was situated. Rita greeted my knock on the door and showed me in to her very nicely furnished sitting room. From where I sat, I could see that her kitchen was equally tidy and well equipped. Tellingly, there was a pile of *House & Garden* magazines on the floor, beside the TV. Rita was clearly proud of her home and had gone to great lengths to make it comfortable. She told me how she'd been raised a Catholic and today attends Mass each week at St John 's Cathedral. A friend picks her up each Sunday and gives her a lift there.

Once she'd offered me a drink and made sure I was comfortable, she told me her story. She spoke with searing honesty and expressed no regret for the way things had turned out. Born in London she'd worked for a bank, commuting to London Bridge daily.

She said there'd usually been a homeless guy sitting at the top of the steps from the tube station. She'd never for one moment thought she would end up in the same situation. 'I thought of them as losers,' she explained. But that's exactly what happened to her. Her parents had moved to Norfolk, and she'd moved up with them. She found a clerical job with a retailer and rented a flat in Norwich.

The following few years brought romance and two sons, which many would have led to life continuing happily ever after. However Rita was not that fortunate. She developed a mental health problem that made it difficult for her to manage money and maintain the family home. She was by now a single parent, and began to struggle.

She had a breakdown, and her two sons were taken into care. Now both adult, she only hears from one, who writes her an annual update on his life. 'He's got a place at Cambridge University,' she told me. 'Isn't that marvellous?' Indeed it is I said, really hoping that one day Rita and her sons can be reunited. She is a lady who now has so much love to give.

But her breakdown led to rent arrears and eventually eviction. With just the clothes she stood up in and nowhere to go, she slept for six weeks in a city centre doorway. She went to a cash-point each morning to withdraw just enough of her benefit money to buy food. She knew that to carry much cash when sleeping rough was just asking to be robbed.

The Salvation Army's ARC project provided a daily breakfast and somewhere to take a shower and do her laundry. This all took place in the spring, so the worst of the bad weather was over, but as Rita said, sleeping rough and spending days in the library, or just walking round, was no fun.

As well as using the bank to withdraw her benefits, she was able to keep her mobile phone charged. This made looking for a job easier and it was at the Job Centre that she was referred to St Martins. They found her a hostel bed, and then a bedsit in a shared house. She told me that she found the hostel easier and did not get along so well with those she found herself sharing a house with.

Now in her mid-50s, life for Rita has never been better than it is now she has a flat at Webster Court. She's saved up to buy items of furniture and for the first time in years, tells me she has no personal debt. Her benefits fund her rent and she has money left over for food and clothing. Most weeks, she is also able to fund an outing, perhaps to a garden centre or the seaside for lunch.

Living at Webster Court gives Rita the stability and security she needs to maintain her mental health. Regular medication keeps things under control and she clearly enjoys her life now. Attending church clearly also plays a key part in her wellbeing. It was telling that she kept attending Mass when living rough. I wonder why nobody there noticed her plight and offered support.

Already Rita has been living at Webster Court for a few years. She will probably still be living there in 30 years' time too; a fact she seems happy about. She's made friends here and loves the courtyard garden where they can sit and chat.

Obviously Rita regrets that she has minimal contact with her two sons. 'If life had turned out differently,' she told me, 'I'd have liked to become a social worker, helping families that are finding things tough.' Perhaps had she been younger, and had her health been better, that could have been possible and she could have become another of the formerly homeless now working in this field.

National statistics suggest that only around 15% of rough sleepers are women. Perhaps they are less likely to walk out than men. Perhaps when a relationship breaks down, it is the men who more usually leave the family home. I wonder how many women there are out there at risk of following in Rita's footsteps?

Robbie

Before I left Webster Court, I had a chat with Robbie, an amenable guy of 74, whose rugged face hints at his past life. Like Rita, Robbie has also lived here for a few years, in his own flat. A bad fall means he now walks with a stick. His mobility scooter is parked outside and as I drove away, having spoken some more with Joy, I saw him driving back from the nearby shop.

Robbie is Scottish and came to Norfolk as a seasonal worker in the holiday camps on the east coast. Norfolk has a good number of these resorts, catering for the many who come to the county each year for their holidays. Many who worked in the camps during the summer, found winter employment in the nearby sugar beet factory at Cantley.

In the early years, Robbie used to travel back to Scotland for the winters. But high living in the summers, particularly drinking, made travelling back north less appealing. He preferred to stay among his new friends and found casual winter work unloading lorries on Norwich Livestock Market. Then in the city centre, in the shadows of the castle, the market was busy and cash-in-hand work easy to get. Robbie quickly built a reputation as a man unafraid of hard work.

It would be true to say that Robbie developed something of a drink problem and often found himself without a bed for the night. He took to sleeping in a bandstand, along with others in a similar situation. They become a tightly knit network, taking it in turns to buy food and especially drink, as each received their dole money on a different day.

I'd already found out, speaking with Stacey who manages

Bishopbridge House, the city's direct access hostel, that when people arrive for the first time, they already know quite a few of the residents. There is a strong sense of community among any city's rough sleepers and Norwich is clearly no exception.

Robbie has been using the services of St Martins for perhaps 30 years. He remembers going to the old night shelter on Oak Street. As Nick, the St Martins trustee we met earlier had already told me, this was very basic and did little more than provide a warmer alternative to sleeping on the street. However on some nights there was not a space in the night shelter, so he returned to the bandstand or perhaps a multi-storey car park, which was more sheltered.

He also explained how when unable to work on the market, he'd taken to begging in the street. 'I sat near a cash machine,' he told me, 'as this seemed to improve my chances.' However he told me he was just as likely to be sworn at or kicked.

Robbie no longer drinks to excess, and appears to have settled to life at Webster Court. Like Rita, he has made friends here and, also like Rita, he expects to see his days out here. A quietly spoken, gentle man with a soft Scottish accent, I warmed to Robbie and enjoyed his company.

I could not help but wonder how many people over the years had missed out by shouting at him, rather than taking the trouble to listen to his story. It seems to me that we are all too busy these days to stop and think and to listen to those we bump into by chance.

I've long been a fan of those unplanned conversations with strangers, but must admit that it's far easier to quickly walk past someone sitting in a shop doorway. Perhaps reading this book will encourage you to say hello, rather than look the other way. We are all human, all different and none of us knows for sure what awaits us in the future.

9

There's light at the end of the tunnel

'It's interesting because people assume that because I'm famous I know all famous people.'
Daniel Radcliffe

I've learned over the years that you can never make assumptions about people. Things are rarely quite as straightforward as they seem and in my experience, people can be too quick to jump to conclusions. For example people never bothered to find out why I failed my 11+ at school. They assumed I was not as bright as those that passed and for a while I believed those assumptions and dutifully failed exam after exam.

Only later in life did I join Mensa and at the age of 64, go to university to study for a Master's degree. Had I been encouraged, supported and my childhood traumas dealt with, life for me could have been very different. Yet today, in our politically correct society, people continue to be conveniently pigeonholed and denied opportunity as a result. We tend to be too quick to make assumptions.

Most people, when they encounter a rough sleeper or beggar on the street, jump to conclusions. It helps you to walk by if you assume they are somehow there as a consequence of their own folly. Yet when you stop and take the trouble to ask, you will hear some amazing stories. Yes, some might be fabricated to encourage you to hand over some money, but most will be true. Try it, but expect to have your assumptions challenged.

My research had quickly told me that rough sleeping is not the end of the line. Most find accommodation, first in a hostel and then a place of their own. In time they find work and in some cases, fame and wealth. In 2008 the singer Ed Sheeran slept under an arch near Buckingham Palace and on Circle Line trains for a while. He wrote a song titled 'Homeless' as a result. When you leave life on the street, the sky really is the limit.

I wanted to meet people who had been homeless in Norwich and made their way back. A little research and some introductions led me to meet some really interesting people. Few who've slept rough want to advertise the fact, but some were prepared to tell me their stories.

Jeremy

Tall, slim and smiling, with piercing brown eyes, Jeremy has an easy manner that invites conversation. Your first impression on meeting him will not be that he has slept rough and now lives in a hostel. Appearances, as I've been learning, can be deceptive. It is always worth taking the time to learn the story behind the face.

Jeremy is currently living at Highwater House, a hostel for

homeless people with addiction, or mental health problems. He has seen terrible things in his life and endured real hardship over the years, but here, for now anyway, he is safe and has a place he can feel valued and call home.

It is early days in his journey back from rough sleeping, and fitting that he should feature first in this chapter. Others will be further down the road, but for Jeremy, memories of living rough are strong and sometimes raw. We met at Highwater House, and Jeremy told me his story.

Jeremy travelled the world when serving in the army. He's seen action in both Afghanistan and Iraq. He did not want to talk too much about his time there, other than to tell me he had seen comrades killed and mutilated. Experiences like that must stay with you for years. I wondered if PTSD was a factor in his spending time sleeping rough? It was not a subject he wanted to talk about so our conversation moved on.

Jeremy has also been a professional jump jockey, a job he enjoyed until he came off a horse one day and landed on his head. This led to several months in hospital. As I know from my own experience of concussion, an acquired brain injury can really hit your mental health. In my own case, it led to some quite severe and very frightening suicidal urges. I chose not to ask if Jeremy's experience had been similar.

His injury however caused him to lose his job riding horses and he decided to come to Norwich to make a fresh start. For whatever reason, he neither was able to find a job, nor a place to live. But being single, and with the benefit of his army training, he decided to rough it for a while until his circumstances improved.

Alcohol became Jeremy's friend during this time. He had the time and found solace in quite literally drowning his sorrows. He's not proud of the fact that his drinking led to begging, and on bad days, to shoplifting. This earned him a week in prison, an experience he looks back on with little regret. It was warmer, more comfortable and with regular meals, things he'd not enjoyed when living rough.

We then talked about what life was really like living rough. The word that came to mind as Jeremy talked was brutal. I got the sense that sleeping in the city centre was dangerous, violent and using the soup kitchen meant risking getting mugged, beaten or even having your food snatched from your hand before you could eat it. Like others, Jeremy talked about how passers-by would shout abuse, kick or beat you and even piss on you if you were asleep. This cannot be the nicest way to be woken up in the small hours.

Jeremy also explained how if you climbed in to your sleeping bag, you could not defend yourself if attacked. He also described how if you'd been begging, other rough sleepers would rob you to get money for drink or drugs. If he had the good fortune to be given any banknotes, they'd be quickly tucked into his sock for safety. He suffered broken bones in attacks; it was interesting to learn that once you'd been patched up at A&E, you'd be discharged back onto the street. I guess discharge to a hostel would slow things down.

As I'd heard from others, many rough sleepers walk out from the city centre to sleep. Jeremy had a place in the woods, where he'd used his army training to create a shelter. Here he could sleep safely, particularly if you were not alone, but with one or two friends. He would light a fire and sometimes catch and cook a rabbit.

I asked why violence was not reported to the police. 'Nobody wants to be branded a grass,' was Jeremy's reply. The rough sleeping community is, I was told, self-policing, with 'street justice' meted out to those that break the unspoken code. Word can spread fast among those living on the streets. It really is quite a jungle out there. There are also undercover policemen, posing as rough sleepers to gather intelligence.

It was a Pathways worker who helped Jeremy start his recovery. He weighed just six and a half stone and was drinking significant volumes of alcohol each day. He spent some time at Bishopbridge House, then moved to Highwater House where I met him. Here he was referred to national charity Change, Grow, Live who helped him with his alcoholism.

Jeremy has made tremendous progress. A healthy diet has seen him return to a normal bodyweight and his drinking is now under control. He can now start to look ahead and plan his future, although there is no pressure on him to leave Highwater; he will only move to a council flat when he is ready.

I asked Jeremy what his message was to readers of this book. 'Tell them that we're not all bad,' he said. 'And that if you give money to a beggar, make sure he's really homeless and not a professional, taking advantage of people's generosity.'

Later, I was made painfully aware of the universality of homelessness. Even after researching this book, I still find it hard to truly believe that I, you, or anyone else could find ourselves living on the street. It just seems such a long way from the comfortable middle class life I lead. Then I met Colin.

Colin

A skilled engineer responsible for quality at a factory making diesel engines, Colin is intelligent, articulate and highly educated. He visited me at my home one Saturday morning. He took a sip of the cup of coffee I'd poured him, and then he sat back and told me his story.

'I had a decent upbringing,' Colin said, 'with wonderful, caring parents who rarely drank and as I was the youngest, they rather spoilt me.' This I realised was a stark contrast to my own upbringing, with an alcoholic father and, as a result, a desperately unhappy mother. It was a shock to realise that Colin's early life was probably much happier than my own.

Circumstances found him starting at a different comprehensive school from the one his friends attended. He was bullied for a while, then toughened up and started to fight back. He said he became known as the 'crazy kid', fearless and perhaps inevitably often in trouble with his teachers.

At 14 Colin discovered alcohol and found that drinking gave him even greater courage to defend himself in the playground. His pocket money was no longer enough to meet his needs, and so he started stealing alcohol from shops. 'One day,' he said ruefully, 'the police arrived at school to arrest me for shoplifting.' This perhaps marked a turning point. Colin soon graduated on to drugs, buying amphetamines from a friend's brother at school.

An engineering apprenticeship followed school; so did cannabis, LSD and hanging round at weekends with a group his father described as 'juvenile delinquents'. Colin found he didn't care what his parents thought and his spare time was spent drinking, doing drugs and fighting. At the age of 18 he hit a policeman, which earned him a 28 day stay at Hollesley Bay, a borstal on the Suffolk coast. 'The staff were tough, mostly forces-trained and discipline was strict,' Colin explained. 'I was only there for four weeks, but that was enough. It made me more cautious about law-breaking. I did not want to go back.'

But Colin did return to prison, although only for a short sentence. By now he was working for a local engineering consultancy, was married and had a daughter. He started selling drugs, as a way of funding his own addiction. He drank less, but only because he needed to be lucid to sell drugs. His marriage broke up and his drug-fueled lifestyle continued. Then one night in a club he was stabbed, almost died and was unable to work for six months.

This cost him his job. A new girlfriend, this time also a drug user, made life a little easier, but his drug usage had reached a level where he was having psychotic episodes and violent outbursts. Colin was now a danger to himself and others.

As Colin explained, skilled engineers are in short supply, so he soon found a better job and managed to perform at work, while also drinking and taking drugs at home. He was well paid, so could afford his habit. On a weekday he was a respected member of the management team in a factory. At weekends he might be in an inner city tower block taking crack cocaine. The contrast was stark and unsustainable. In 2015 he returned to Norfolk and a job at the same engineering consultancy. But his relationship had once more ended and he was living in B&Bs.

Then his money ran out and for a time, he slept in a city centre shop doorway. A security guard who'd nabbed him stealing a bottle of wine recommended he attend Alcoholics Anonymous. The Police Community Support Officer who came out and the shop security guard spoke. The shop decided not to press charges and the PCSO, Lynne, bought him a meal in a nearby café.

Those simple acts of kindness prompted a change in Colin. He took the advice, attended both Alcoholics Anonymous and Narcotics Anonymous and today, just four years later, Colin once more has a good job and his own place to live. After meeting me he was off to collect a set of wheels he had just bought for his classic car, a Ford Cortina.

St Martins helped him too, with courses at Under 1 Roof helping him to manage his previously uncontrollable urges. He also has the incentive of knowing that if he gets arrested, he will be straight back in prison as he is currently on licence for a knife crime committed in 2017. Because by then his recovery was well under way, he was given a two-year suspended sentence.

Prison is not somewhere Colin ever wants to go again. He talked about sharing a cell with a man he hardly knew, who would smoke heroin in the cell before turning in for the night. But staying off drugs and drink, Colin knows, can never be taken for granted. That perhaps is why he volunteers with St Martins, going into schools to tell his story to students.

He hopes that this will help them avoid making the mistakes he made. He doesn't want to see today's young people endure the hardships he's endured. He also knows that because he was raised in a comfortable middle-class family and held down a responsible job, even when taking drugs, that his talks shatter the perception that drugs and homelessness only happen to other people. The truth is, that it can happen to anyone.

Tony

I wanted to meet a few more people who had slept rough, and were now housed and leading what you might call a normal life. On my travels researching this book I'd met Tony who is the Norwich Coordinator for Hope into Action, a fascinating national charity that enables churches to play a part in housing the homeless.

We'd first encountered one another at a meeting and Tony agreed to take me to visit some of the people the charity was supporting in Norwich. By way of preparation, I took a look at the charity's website. I could quickly see how Hope into Action was different from other hostel or housing providers. People housed by this charity benefit from the support of a welcoming church congregation.

The model is simple. A church is matched with a house and that house then let to people who have been homeless. The house is usually leased from a buy-to-let landlord who accepts a below market rent because they value what the charity achieves. A house might be let to two or three single people, or a family. A support worker makes sure the tenant has help when they need it and the host church provides friendship and often a volunteer mentor. It is wonderfully simple, although I suspect like every other provider I met, problems do occur.

We met at Tony's office in the city centre. He'd promised to drive me to the house where two of his tenants had agreed to meet. Tony had not always worked in the charity sector; he'd had a career in the Fleet Air Arm of the Royal Navy first. He'd trained as an aircraft engineer and had for a time also been a pilot. Landing a plane on a moving aircraft carrier sounded like risky work.

Tony was not new to working with vulnerable people. 'The Navy attracts people looking to escape from an unhappy life,' he told me, 'and when at sea, you are all living in a confined space, so have to support each other.' I could see how someone wanting to make a fresh start could join up, in the hope of leaving their problems behind. Life is rarely that simple.

We talked about the people his organisation has helped since he's been involved. None it seems had served in the Navy, but quite a few had Army backgrounds. This Tony explained, was probably because in the Navy, you're not involved in close combat as is so often the case for soldiers on the front line. I'd already met one former soldier who had slept rough and I suspected had suffered from post-traumatic stress disorder (PTSD).

Our conversation continued as we walked to Tony's car and drove to one of the houses they have in Norwich. All are within walking distance of the city centre, but it was raining and this was the furthest out. Tony told me something of the two men I was going to meet. Both had agreed to talk with me and I was looking forward to hearing how in practice the involvement of a church made a difference.

We arrived at the house and Tony knocked on the door. There was no answer so he rang one of the men on his mobile. Annoyingly, he had gone into the city centre on an errand and so was not around; nor was the other man. Tony offered to rearrange for another day, but I said no. It was, I thought, important to illustrate the point that people who have been homeless will often have different priorities to a writer.

10

Discovering one's potential

*'Learn from yesterday, live for today, hope for tomorrow. The
important thing is not to stop questioning.'*
Albert Einstein

Many of those I met while writing this book have turned
their lives around. They've left behind the challenges that
caused them to become rough sleepers and gone on to make
something of their lives. None though could be described
as young, and some were a good few years older even than
me.

Of course it is never too late to make a fresh start, but
being in my mid-60s, I am very aware that life does not go
on for ever. I know that the day will come when the good
health and active lifestyle I currently enjoy will change.
Hopefully the deterioration will be slow and gradual, but I
know that inevitably, in 15 years' time, like it or not, I will
be an old man.

I was reflecting on this awful subject at the Forum in
Norwich one day, when Tim, the CEO of YMCA Norfolk,
strode up to me and asked me how I was and what was

my current project. He's someone I've come to know and respect over the years he's been in Norwich. I told him I was writing this book. 'Will we feature?' he asked, 'because we have some amazing young people who have experienced rough sleeping and would love to be interviewed.' How could I refuse?

As I knew from mentoring an ex-offender of a similar age to myself, the delight at witnessing someone changing their ways and taking on new challenges, can be tinged with sadness because they have wasted so much of their life in prison. Changing young lives must be very rewarding. A date was arranged to visit one of the YMCA hostels in Norwich. I also did a little research.

YMCA stands for Young Men's Christian Association. It was founded in 1844 by a 22 year old draper called George Williams. He created a safe haven where young men could escape the hurly burly and hazards of life in Victorian London to meet and study the Bible together.

The organisation grew through the 19th century, establishing reading rooms, gyms and even a holiday park, where young men could escape the city altogether for a break. The YMCA has evolved over the years in response to demand for services. It no longer holds Bible classes, although I suspect something could be arranged if a youngster asked. It remains a Christian charity. For many years the YMCA has also supported young women as well as young men.

Nationally the YMCA provides a home and lots of support to more than 18,000 young people aged 16-25. There is no doubt that putting a roof over a young person's head is a vital first step in turning round a troubled life. As

Tim explained: 'Our mission is to enable transformation in the lives of young people and we provide housing because this aim is impossible for a young person who is surviving day by day, whether insecurely housed or on the streets.'

Tim went on to remind me that what we see on the streets is the tip of a very large iceberg. Many are vulnerably housed, moving from friend to friend and sleeping on the sofa. As others told me, you can soon outstay your welcome, even when put up by members of your own family.

The YMCA provides hostel beds, supported lodgings, where the young person stays with a family, and shared housing, where people can develop the confidence and skills they need to have a place of their own.

While you can marry at 16 and vote at 18, scientists will tell you that full maturity is not achieved until around the age of 25. The YMCA therefore supports young people as they emerge from the turbulence of adolescence until adulthood has become fully established. It's a crucial stage of anyone's life.

It came as a shock to realise that young people can find themselves sleeping rough. I realised that I had always assumed that parents, grandparents or other family members would take sufficient interest in a young person's life to prevent them becoming homeless. But this was another example of my middle class roots showing. The sad fact is that not all parents remain interested in their offspring. Sometimes the problems they themselves are facing are just too overwhelming to make parenting possible.

Then of course there are children raised by the state, because for whatever reason they have no family of their own. I was reminded of Rita, who I described in Chapter Eight who had both of her children taken away. This was a consequence of her then quite severe mental health problems. Her sons were fostered and only when they reached the age of 18 did they have the opportunity to rekindle their relationship with their mother.

Local authorities often commission private companies to provide supported accommodation for young care leavers. There was a recent press expose of one such home in Norfolk that was far from appropriate. The local paper, the *Eastern Daily Press*, published shocking images of what appeared to be appalling accommodation into which young care leavers were being moved.

I realised that young people, just as much as anyone older, could become homeless and find themselves sleeping rough. I arranged to visit a YMCA hostel in Norwich and speak with some of the young people living there.

Situated facing the bus station, facing where I habitually catch the park and ride bus, the hostel is fairly new. It has a café that faces out to the station. It's where many drivers go for their lunch break. The café also caters for the hostel's residents. I'd also used the café, preferring to patronise a charity than a chain store outlet. They serve nice cake!

The entrance to the hostel is at the rear of the building and I had to ask in the café where it was. I guess it makes sense not to have the front door opening on to a busy bus station! But it meant that while I was familiar with the building, as soon as I walked round the side, I felt I was entering an unknown world.

I was greeted by the team that work here, shown into a

common room and introduced by Abi, one of the support workers, to my two interviewees.

Beth

Life has not been good for Beth, but her smile and cheerfulness suggested a degree of pragmatism in her approach to life. Just 22 years old, she has had three children, all of whom were taken into care. Her partner is serving a prison sentence and several friends have died of drug overdoses. Estranged from her family, Beth spent three years living on the streets before securing a bed at this YMCA hostel. Beth has squeezed a lifetime's bad luck into just a few years.

Born in Norfolk, Beth left home when her parents split up. With her boyfriend she travelled to Weston-Super-Mare where they took a short lease on a flat. Both were working and life for a time was good. Her boyfriend had developed a drug habit, and Beth's mental health was far from robust.

When the lease on their flat ended, they could neither find nor afford a new place so slept rough. They moved round a bit, looking for work and sleeping rough. 'We were able to claim benefits,' she explained, 'but it was not enough to enable us to get a place.' What money they had went on food, clothing and inevitably drugs. Medical care is hard to obtain too when you're living rough. So too is access to contraception. The couple's three children were all conceived and born when they were sleeping rough, or in temporary hostel accommodation. Each child was taken away for adoption within days of being born. No mother wants to lose her child and to lose three over three years must have been tough.

Beth told me she has 'letterbox contact' with her three children. I had to look this up, and found that it is a formal arrangement by which birth parents can be kept in touch with their children's progress. When they reach 18, they will have the opportunity to make contact, but that must feel like a lifetime away.

Having heard from others how rough life can be on the street, I asked Beth how she managed. She told me how while men could be aggressive and rude, women were more sympathetic, often stopping to offer food or money. It was a relief I'm sure for Beth to finally find a safe place to live at the YMCA hostel.

According to the YMCA Norfolk website, a hostel bed is provided to those that have completed a 'Hostel Accommodation Form'. In Norwich, referrals are usually made by the Pathways team, who reach out to and support those that are sleeping rough. This was how Beth came to be at the YMCA.

But what brought her back to Norfolk I wondered? 'My granddad lives in Norwich,' Beth told me, 'and I thought he might be able to help us.' However for whatever reason, he could not offer her accommodation and so she slept rough for a time, before securing a bed in the hostel where we met.

Her boyfriend, father of their three children, was in prison for drug-related violent crime. I did not ask for details, being more concerned about how Beth was coping without him. She clearly missed having him around and was visiting him at Norwich Prison just twice a month, which is as often as the rules allow.

It became apparent talking with Beth, that here, just feet from the bus station, people were living in a very different world to the one I usually inhabit. Beth talked about people she'd known locally who had died from drug overdoses. She talked about the fact that heroin was cheaper to buy if you buy several wraps at a time. She talked about crime, and the street law by which those who are homeless police themselves.

Beth had explained that she had trouble with her mental health. You might say this is no surprise, when you consider the life she has led this past few years. But one cannot make assumptions and we never know if poor mental health is the cause, or consequence of family rejection and homelessness.

I asked if Beth hoped to find work now that she had someone to say. She felt that her health would make this difficult. In common with many I met, Beth was not able to imagine the better life she will probably be living in a few years' time. She is still young, and so has most of her life ahead of her. Many have moved on from her situation to get a place of their own, a job and family. But ask any young person to imagine what their life will be like in five or 10 years' time, and they will struggle. Few of Beth's age have made long-term plans or can predict how their future will be.

As our conversation was drawing to a close, a young man called Josh appeared in the doorway. He'd also been invited to meet me. He appeared restless and wandered around the room a bit, making himself a hot drink and weighing up if I looked like a guy he would want to talk with. I passed that test, and he came over, shook my hand and sat down.

Josh

The story Josh told me was not unusual. He had got into trouble with the police for stealing food from his guardian. The circumstances that led to him being in the care of a guardian and what prompted him to steal food I suspect could form a story by themselves. I chose not to probe but to ask instead about the time Josh had spent living rough.

Like Beth, Josh had clearly not had a happy upbringing. Mental health problems mean he'd been sectioned at the age of 17, and spent time in hospital. This episode however is very much in his past. From our conversation I could see that he takes a keen interest in the world around him. His past is clearly behind him and a brighter future lies ahead.

For a time, Josh had lived in a garage on an industrial estate near the city centre. He'd been quite happy living by himself and had enjoyed the independence it gave him. But then the owner put a lock on the door, and so Josh found himself sleeping rough. He had nowhere else to go.

Luckily Josh was referred to the YMCA and now has somewhere to sleep. It somehow seems more shocking when a young man barely in his 20s ends up on the street. How could life turn out so badly for one so young? Regrettably Josh's story is far from unique, although most who find themselves sleeping rough are older.

Perhaps inevitably, drugs have featured in Josh's life for some time. I don't think he was a heavy user, but clearly had friends who were. Like Beth, he was able to tell me things about the world of drugs I did not know.

For example, I learned why smuggling drugs into prison was so popular. 'Drugs that cost you £50 on the street, have a value of perhaps £1,000 when inside,' he explained. I guess it's the simple economics of supply and demand, although I still wonder how people manage to take drugs in and pass them over to a prisoner dealer.

Josh also gave me a fresh perspective on the link between drug use and violent crime. Heroin use can cause lasting heart damage, as well as suppressing adrenalin uptake. So taking risks, for example carrying out a crime, with the risk of being caught, can stimulate adrenalin production in ways that are no longer possible in any other way. I guess it puts robbing a shop on a par with riding a rollercoaster, except of course there is no rollercoaster in Norwich city centre!

I was also a little taken aback when Josh said 'everyone' knew where the drug dealers lived. He was surprised that one he knew, who traded 'openly' in the city centre, had not been arrested. He also invited me to visit a crack-den with him; an invitation I politely declined.

Streetwise is I suppose a word you could use to describe Josh. He knows where the drug lines run, the going rate for heroin and crack, and takes for granted the fact that organised crime delivers drugs inside the local prison to order.

I was surprised, and when I left the hostel and crossed the bus station to catch my park and ride bus, was again struck by how close the hostel and bus station were. Yet for those waiting for their bus home, the world described by those I'd met at the hostel was completely alien. Most would be shocked to hear what went on under their noses in the city they thought they knew. This of course is one of the reasons why I decided to write this book.

11

Can we ever solve the problem?

'Life is about taking steps that move you forwards.'
John Bird

People have always found themselves homeless. Inevitably, there will always be those who through no fault of their own find themselves on the streets. However the nature of homelessness is changing. In the 19th century, it was fairly straightforward. You had no job, no money and without a welfare state, little hope. The Vagrancy Act meant you kept moving too, so people continuously tramped from place to place in search of work, food and shelter.

In Chapter Eight, I introduced you to Robbie, who lived on the streets 30 years ago. He told me that then, drinking was the way you dealt with the feelings of desperation. Of course many also had a mental health problem, but people did not seem to have the complexity of challenge that seems to be the case today.

We all read in the newspapers about the growing drug problem. But it was a shock to discover that crack cocaine and heroin can cost £10 or less a shot. I'd always thought drugs were expensive. Of course they still are if you are living rough, although if you can get free food and a hostel bed, then what benefits money you do get can supplement what you make by begging or stealing. Funding an addiction on the street is not that difficult.

What this means for those working in the homelessness sector is that the people they work with are now more likely to have complex problems that take a great deal of unpicking. We cannot underestimate the impact of this trend towards complexity. Most of us have experience of friends and family developing a mental health or drink problem. But few of us will understand the challenges created when someone experiences a drug-induced psychotic episode.

Those working at the front line, be they charity, council or health workers, or volunteers dishing out soup and sandwiches, now face very real dangers. The people they are helping will be living with often quite severe mental health problems, or drug addictions which combine to make them a risk to both themselves and others. It's not unusual for the police to be called when violence breaks out as people are being fed in the city centre.

One former rough sleeper told me how he'd lost three friends to suicide. While we are all enjoying our comfortable lifestyles, some are living through Armageddon right under our noses. I wanted to make this final chapter a positive one. It was a tall order, but my research did lead to a hopeful interview.

Iain

Although he's not experienced homelessness himself, Iain speaks with real passion on the subject. 'It gets under your skin, but in a good way,' he told me. 'I've worked in this sector for 18 years and don't expect to leave it,' he added. It was a friend who did a shift in a St Martins hostel who introduced him to this line of work. Iain soon found himself leaving his sales job to work at St Martins.

We talked about the complex issues that lead to many people finding themselves on the street. Childhood neglect, perhaps time in the care system and the failure of those in the system to provide the support needed. Iain works with those that are hardest to help.

Iain explained how The Prison Reform Trust had found that while only 1% of children go into care, half of the youngster held in custody had been in care. When you look at the adult prison population, one in four was once in care. A prison sentence is often a passport to rough sleeping. Many on release have nowhere to go, sleep rough and inevitably run the risk of returning to jail.

To me it seems obvious to provide more effective support for young people in care, and to ensure that everyone released from prison has a bed to sleep in that night. But as Iain explained, it's not that simple. I'd already found out myself that councils simply don't have the money to invest in schemes that can save them money later. And of course we must never forget the misery and despair that can be the consequence of inadequate support in early life.

Iain knows his subject. He's read widely, attended conferences and is in the process of writing a book. He describes the hostel where he works as a 'psychologically informed environment'. This sounded complicated, so I asked Iain to explain what this phrase means. I'm familiar with the world of psychotherapy, but this I was told, is quite different.

A psychologically informed environment is one that has five elements. These are psychological awareness; the environment; evidence and enquiry; rules, roles and responsiveness; and finally staff support and training. This all seemed rather complex, which of course homelessness is.

I did a little research and found a useful article on the Homelessness Link website. Essentially all people think, feel and believe in similar ways. We're hardwired to respond in certain ways to the world around us. If past experience has damaged us in some way, as is often the case for those who end up living rough, then emotional responses can be distorted or exaggerated.

A psychologically informed environment then is one where people work in ways that recognise the potential impact on people who have been damaged. This means creating familiar routines and minimising the unexpected. Routine, patience and tolerance seems to sum it up. It rather reminded me of the way care homes manage people with dementia.

As Iain explained, many find themselves sleeping rough as a consequence of childhood abuse. Certainly the signs professionals recognise as potential indicators that a child is being abused – aggression, being withdrawn and avoiding interaction, substance abuse, bullying and poor personal hygiene – are also behaviours displayed by many of those Iain works with.

Iain works at Highwater House, the care home we visited earlier that supports people with a history of substance abuse, poor mental health and often both. These are the most troubled members of our society and as I discovered when I met Angela who manages the home, many have been turned away by other providers.

In common with most I met, Iain was keen to point out that nobody volunteers to become homeless. 'It is,' he told me, 'a frightening experience in which you can feel completely alone in the world. I learned that most rough sleepers carry a knife because they fear attack. Iain wasn't sure how many would have the confidence to use one though.

It is perhaps no surprise that sometimes someone has a psychotic episode and needs to be admitted to a psychiatric hospital. Iain's organisation works closely with its local mental health trust. Even so, it can take a while for someone to be taken to the safety of a ward when it becomes necessary for them to be sectioned. At the time of writing, the local mental health trust is in special measures, which does not help.

So the fact is that homelessness is not a problem that needs to be fixed, because it can never be fixed. There will always be people who for whatever reason find themselves sleeping rough. Most will find somewhere to sleep with family or friends. What can change though is society's approach to those who find themselves without a place to sleep.

Let me give you an example. Joe is in his mid-20s, married with a toddler and a baby. He started his own business, and the pressure of this, together with the worry about supporting a second child, led to the breakdown of his marriage. His business did not grow as he had planned; he fell out with his business partner, the business failed and he took a low paid job driving a parcel delivery van.

His wife asked him to leave the family home and he was too proud to ask his parents to take him in. He slept in his van at night for a while, until a friend offered him a room. He remains vulnerably housed and is one of the many we don't see living on the streets, but who could find themselves there very easily.

I knew that Joe's marriage was in trouble. I also knew that his business was failing. But I did not put two and two together and wonder if he was struggling to find somewhere to live. It's not something you think about unless you or someone close to you loses their home. I've been happily married for 37 years and been a home owner for 40 years. Joe's plight is far removed from my own experience.

So I did not ask and Joe did not volunteer that he was in trouble. I think we all need to make time to keep in touch with the people we know. Furthermore, if our intuition suggests that all is not well, we should ask outright. Too many I suspect don't ask difficult questions because they are unwilling to offer money or accommodation themselves, and want to avoid the embarrassment of having to say no.

Having spoken with people who have become homeless, and had to resort to living on the street, the single biggest thing that would have helped them is to be greeted and treated as a fellow human being.

Almost everyone I spoke to who had been on the street spoke about the abuse and violence they'd encountered. Not at the hands of other rough sleepers, or even drug dealers, but from often well-dressed people, who seem to think it's clever to abuse someone who is down on their luck.

So how can you and I make a difference to the lives of those blighted by homelessness and sleeping rough? How should we respond when asked for money by someone sitting in a shop doorway? How can the businesses we work for or the places where we worship get involved and provide practical help? These are all good questions, to which there is no easy or straightforward answer.

Researching and writing this book has challenged my assumptions. I thought I understood the problems of homelessness, but quickly discovered that I had a lot to learn. I've met some amazing people, and encountered shocking misery on the streets of my local city. A walk out with a Pathways outreach team took me to scenes of filth and squalor, just a few yards from busy streets.

To help you decide how you should respond to home-lessness, here are 10 things you might like to consider. Remember, though, that it is not just the big things that make a difference. Even a smile and a hello can brighten the day of someone living on the streets. Kindness costs you nothing more than a little time.

1 Remember that we are all the same under the surface

A few years ago, I and 3,000 others took off our clothes, painted our bodies blue and posed naked for the American photographer Spencer Tunick. That experience, on a chilly summer morning in Hull, helped me see that when deprived of clothes and possessions, we really are all just the same.

When you encounter a rough sleeper, there is an imbalance, because you have your home, job, car, family and clean clothes. They might have just the clothes they're standing up in, no relationships, job, money or anything at all.

But don't be embarrassed, or feel guilty about this. Just put the differences to one side and make time to say hello and take an interest if they want to talk. They can feel very lonely and isolated, even sitting on a busy street, because most of us will just look away and walk by.

2 Don't judge; just do

Someone on my travels made the point that when a beggar asks for money, you assume she or he will waste it on drugs. But when a businessman in a suit charges you for a professional service, you don't give a thought to how he will spend his fee. He might well have a drink or drug habit; be addicted to gambling, or be beating his wife.

As I discovered, rough sleepers come from all walks of life. That person who stops you in the street might have been raised in care and failed at school. But they might also have a PhD and have been to public school. You really cannot make assumptions about the people you meet, on the street, or anywhere else for that matter.

It is your call if you decide to give some change to someone begging. There is no right or wrong answer, although many choose to buy a copy of the *Big Issue*, or give to a homelessness charity instead. What matters is that you do something, rather than pretend you haven't noticed.

3 Volunteer

There are many opportunities for you to give some time to help those working in this field. The organisations working with homeless people welcome volunteer help. You can mentor someone living in a hostel, help distribute meals on the street, help with administration, or simply take part in a street collection, shaking a tin and talking with the public. Councils and charities can only do so much; volunteers can make all the difference to those we are all trying to help.

I know from first-hand experience that using your expertise and experience to volunteer is hugely rewarding. For example I mentor a vulnerable man who has been in prison. We meet most weeks, talking about his hopes, fears and the practical challenges of finding a council flat so that he can leave the hostel in which he is living.

Seeing his confidence grow, which in turn helped him gain a job, and seeing his delight at securing a flat of his own, has been worth every moment I have spent with him. It has helped me see how fortunate I am to live such a comfortable life.

Volunteering can also help you develop new skills and experiences that can help develop your career. That is why many employers will give their staff time off during the working week to volunteer.

4 Become a donor

Too many people use charity shops as a convenient place to dump stuff they no longer want. But look a little harder at the clutter you have accumulated over the years. Do you have things that others would find useful, but you no longer have need for? In Norwich, St Martins have a 'donation station' where you can give clothing that homeless people will value. Your city will have something similar I'm sure.

Of course many give money to people begging on the street. I'll not encourage or discourage you from doing this, but suggest that regular giving to a homelessness charity might make a bigger difference. Remember that if you are a tax-payer, charities can often claim Gift Aid on your donation.

For the bold, there are opportunities to organise or take part in a sponsored event. Training for a and running in an organised race can boost your fitness, and create an opportunity for family, friends and colleagues to sponsor your efforts. Businesses can organise sponsored activities too, involving customers and suppliers as well as employees.

5 Offer accommodation

I know one lady who allowed a homeless person to sleep in her conservatory. This is perhaps not the wisest thing to do; to be brutally honest, this can put you at risk. But offering lodgings to a young person leaving care, with the support of an organisation such as the YMCA, can give them a very real chance to get their life back on track. What's more, your expenses are usually covered.

On a larger scale, some charities welcome the opportunity to rent an otherwise empty house, and provide shared accommodation to people leaving hostel accommodation. You get a market rent, unless you choose to charge less, and your property is well managed. We all know there is a housing shortage, and private rented flats or shared houses can make a real difference.

6 Give people jobs

You will remember Colin's story in Chapter Nine. He was a skilled engineer who was able to secure a job with a former employer, after a two-year break to deal with his addiction. He said that there is a shortage of people with his skills so getting a job was not too difficult. But even then, it required a leap of faith from his employer to give him a chance.

We all change and evolve over time, yet employers are swayed more by past experience than future prospects. If you've hit a bad patch and been out of work for any reason, it can be really hard to get a job. If that bad patch involved sleeping rough, drink or drugs, then it can be extremely difficult to find a job.

If you are an employer or manager, think for a moment about how you recruit and why. People who have endured extreme hardship and are now seeking a job will be resilient, determined and may have learned new skills, perhaps in prison. Everybody deserves a second chance; can you give someone the opportunity to put their past behind then and shine working for your organisation?

7 Listen to a story

Many homelessness charities, including St Martins in Norwich, can provide speakers with lived experience to talk to groups. Personal testimony can be a powerful way to make school and other groups learn about the dangers of drink, drugs and crime.

Reading this book is giving you an insight into the world of rough sleeping. Why not follow that up by hearing the story of someone who has been there? Hearing the story of someone who has been homeless will tick boxes if you are a teacher, but more importantly, it can challenge assumptions and increase understanding of the problem.

8 Support your local foodbank

There is a foodbank in every town and city. People that use foodbanks may not be homeless, but they will be living in poverty and often vulnerably housed. If you have a food business, give food that would otherwise be wasted to your local food bank, or a group that feed homeless people.

Remember that for every person sleeping rough, there will be 50 more relying on the goodwill of friends, family or colleagues. People that use foodbanks will often be facing the stark choice between buying food to eat and paying their rent. One of the biggest causes of homelessness is eviction from a private sector rented flat or house.

9 Lobby for change

There are a million and one issues about which you can campaign. Homelessness is just one of them, but if you take the trouble to explore it, you may find yourself moved to act. Social media and press friendly publicity stunts can, if well targeted, allow a small number of people to make millions aware of, and concerned about an issue close to your heart.

Remember that peaceful protest is far more effective than that which damages people or property. Mahatma Gandhi once said that you have to 'be the change you want to see'. In other words, if an aspect of homelessness touches you, think about how you can safely and effectively highlight the change you want to see, through peaceful protest or lobbying politicians you may know.

10 Start a project

I don't mean duplicate existing provision, or set out to compete and perhaps be better than what already exists. Before even thinking about that, you need to take the time and trouble to talk with those providing services in your town or city and really, really understand why they operate as they do.

But those conversations can identify specific gaps in provision that you can usefully plug. My own Quaker Meeting has secured a small grant, that will be matched by Friends' own giving, to create a fund that will guarantee private sector tenancies of those with no recourse to public funds. In Norwich, there are only a few people who find themselves homeless and do not qualify for state support. But we can and will help those people.

Any project you start must be sustainable, practical and capable of being managed next year, with the same enthusiasm your team have for it today.

I hope this list has inspired you to see homelessness in a different light. As I've said several times, you don't have to do big things to make a difference. You just have to recognise that the rough sleeper you encounter in the street is vulnerable, probably afraid, perhaps hungry and unwell. Treat them with kindness and compassion, because they did not choose to be there.

Acknowledgements

It is customary for an author to acknowledge the many people who helped make a book possible. Naturally I want to do that, thanking in particular those whose generosity has funded this book. These include Smith and Pinching, Mattressman, Gascoynes and the Missing Kind and all those listed on the following page, who supported our crowdfunding campaign. Two named funds within Norfolk Community Foundation also gave grants, but asked to remain anonymous. I am grateful for their support too.

This means that when someone buys a copy of this book, either in a shop or online, most if not all of the price they pay will go straight to St Martins, helping fund the brilliant work they do with homeless people.

I've written quite a few books now, but am grateful to both my wife Belinda, who proof read every page, and Keiron Pim who then professionally and thoroughly copy-edited the book before it went near the typesetter.

But most importantly, I want to thank the amazing people who gave me their time, told me their stories and kindly agreed that I could share those stories with you. I only hope that you enjoyed reading about the people I met as much as I enjoyed talking with them. Please, when you next encounter someone who is sleeping rough in your city, don't ignore them. Even a smile or a nod is better than pretending they don't exist.

Supporters

A special thank you to the following people who supported the crowdfunding campaign and so made this book possible.

Adrian Ashton

Anne Aves

Tony Barber

Alex Begg

Iain Boag

Milee Brambleby

Hugh Callacher,
Missing Kind,
www.missingkind.org

Tim Carr

Tony Clifton

Glyn Cotton

Dan Harris

Alison Holmes

Andrew Howe

Mary Lawson

Chris & Sue Liles

Janet O'Keefe

Su Johnston

David Patey

Graham Pentelow

Chris Reeve, Gascoynes,
www.gascoynes.co.uk

Jo Salter

Sue Sharpe

Jade Leigh Smith

Michal Zak

About the author

Robert Ashton is a social entrepreneur, author and campaigner. Redundancy in 1990 introduced him to self-employment. Since then he's worked independently, sometimes with a team but more usually on his own. Much of his work in recent years has involved creating sustainable ventures that can help people overcome the barriers society has placed in their way.

A Quaker, Robert is driven by a strong sense of social justice. He has always been angered by the way our society unthinkingly puts people in pigeonholes and excludes them from opportunity. Failing his 11+ meant an assumption that Robert was incapable of academic achievement. At college he learned how to milk cows, castrate pigs and plough a field.

Only in 2019, after he had finished writing this book, did Robert attend university for the first time, studying for an MA in Biography & Creative Non-Fiction at UEA.

Having spent a summer exploring homelessness, Robert now knows that behind every person you encounter asking for change on the street there is a story. Those stories deserve to be told. All you have to do is stop for a while, ask the question and listen.

www.robertashton.co.uk